Build to Grow

14 THOUGHT LEADERS DELIVER
ENGAGEMENT STRATEGIES
FOR THE C-SUITE

Michael Alf, Ian Bosler, Karol Clark,
Jerry Dreessen, Niki Faldemolaei,
Barry Gumaer Sr., Joe (JT) Ippolito,
Miguel de Jesús, Steve Laurvick,
Sharon MacLean, Stephen Saber,
Olivier Taupin, Melodie Rush, Pat Ziemer

Build To Grow / Intertype
1st Edition
ISBN   978-0-9874466-8-8

Ordering Information
Quantity sales. Special discounts are available on quantity purchases by corporations, associations, and others. For details, contact the "Special Sales Department" at the address above or any of the individual contributors.

Authors
Michael Alf, Ian Bosler, Karol Clark, Jerry Dreessen, Niki Faldemolaei, Barry Gumaer Sr., Joe (JT) Ippolito, Miguel de Jesús, Steve Laurvick, Sharon MacLean, Stephen Saber, Olivier Taupin, Melodie Rush, Pat Ziemer

Editor
Mary VanMeer

Forward

by Kevin Harrington

Inventor of the Infomercial, Original Shark on Shark Tank, "As Seen on TV" pioneer, Chairman of Star Shop, CEO-Kevin Harrington Enterprises & HBD, Recognized as the most highly successful entrepreneur in the history of business growth and development.

Viewers and followers of the Hit TV series Shark Tank are familiar with my work and participation in the growth of the program.

What helped business owners and entrepreneurs on the show to overcome and evaluate, was the review and discussion of the critical business elements that prevented them from accelerated growth, personal development, and ultimately success in their chosen fields.

I have developed a sharp sense of what it takes to be successful.

and am passionate about entrepreneurs. My wish is to have them succeed and grow. I have a finely tuned sense of the strategies and tactics that can win. I also have sense of the things that are necessary for growth;

Personal Branding, Brand Marketing, Practice of The Pitch, and Finding and Raising capital. As I like to say in the Practice the Pitch teaching phase: Tease, Please, and Seize.

When I read the manuscript for "Build To Grow", I knew these authors were smart and talented with their timely insights and strategies. It is an important book, with visionary and transformational topics, that will impact business as we know it, to evolve into the next generation of corporate, individual and entrepreneurial business success.

These contributing authors, are a part of a Mastermind Group of skilled professional who work on discussing and providing solutions to some the toughest issues facing business owners today. The content of this book will provide excellent viewpoints on outsourcing those things that are not aligned with your core business; or are simply not good at doing. But are strategies, policies and programs that still need to be done, in order to consistently grow and in some cases transform your business.

The book, *Build to Grow – 14 Thought Leaders Deliver Engagement Strategies to Grow Your Business,* can serve as the foundation for that growth.

Full details on the book, its authors, and a list of free book bonuses is available now at www.BuildToGrowBook.com. The authors will share insights on a number of topics, including:

- Five leaps to rapidly deflate ballooning healthcare costs, and catapult employee productivity, retention, and brand loyalty.
- How to design brand messaging that captivates the hearts and minds of laser-targeted groups of customers and prospects.
- 10 proven, tested, and ready-to-implement online strategies for the social CEO to transform your ready-aim-fire corporate social media plan into a well-oiled machine with a 3:1 or better ROI.
- How to design brand messaging that captivates the hearts and minds of laser-targeted groups of customers and prospects.

And much more...

You owe to yourself, your customers and your employees to take a look at the many strategies and ideas offered by this team.

Best wishes to you and your leadership team in the coming year.

Kevin Harrington
Inventor of the Infomercial, Original Shark on Shark Tank, "As Seen on TV" pioneer, Chairman of Star Shop, CEO-Kevin Harrington Enterprises & HBD.

Contents

How We Retain Information
How to Train Your EQ Brain
My Story
Contact Miguel de Jesús
Bonus Material
Biography
Guiding Statement

Operationalizing Reputation Management
How to Respond to an Online-Reputation Crisis
Update Company Skeleton Profile
Maintain Your Social Media Profiles
Reputation Management: What Does Your Online Presence Say to Prospects?
Link to Positive Content
What Is Online Reputation Management?
Using Analytics
How to Build and Protect Your Digital Reputation
Contact Joe (JT) Ippolito
Biography

What Is a Webinar?
Productive Employees
Lifelong Customers
The rest of the story…
Connect with Melodie Rush
Bonus Material
Biography

Chapter Synopsis
What About Risk Management?
Age of Authenticity

Stage 1: Mindset
Stage 2: Know Your people
Bonus Material
Biographies
Sharon MacLean
Olivier G. Taupin

Customer Retention Methodologies
Beginnings and Fundamentals
Impact of Video
Customer Engagement
Video Techniques: What They Are with Benefits
Webcasts / Videocasts / Livecasts / Intranet Broadcasts (Live and Archived)
Podcasts (Audio and/or Video)
Webinars
Video Newsletters (Information, Entertainment, Education, and Sales)
Video Blogs (Contextual Information)
Video Testimonials (How Lives/Businesses Are Being Changed)
Video Bookcasts (Authority-Positioning Vehicle with Interactive Inclusions)
Video-Filled Events – Major Productions (Widescreen); Webstreams (Live and Archived)
Video Publishing Using Social Media
Regularly-Scheduled Video Broadcasts
Multimedia Messaging Services
Contact Barry D. Gumaer, Sr.
Bonus Material
Biography
Guiding Statement

Multiple-Source Platforms
Multi-Source Strategy

Implementation
Certification Case Study
Contact Pat Ziemer
Bonus Material
Biography

So What Exactly Is a Virtual Summit?
3 Myths about Virtual Summits
1. Virtual Summits No Longer Work
2. No Interaction
3. You Cannot Reach the Audience
Four Ways to Get Started with Creating a Virtual Summit
Step 1. What Is a Potential Virtual Summit (Theme) for Your
Business?
Step 2. What Are Potential Speakers for Your Summit?
Step 3. Potential Models
Step 4. Learn How to Run a Virtual Summit or Find Somebody
Who Can Help
Contact Michael Alf
Bonus Material
Biography

The Digital Publication
Content Creation
Content Curation
Content Distribution
Content Syndication
Analytics
Conclusion
Contact Stephen Saber
Bonus Material
Biography

7 Monetization Strategies to Convert Your Existing Content into
Cash
1. Multicast
2. Livecast
3. Podcast
4. Bookcast
5. Mobilecast
6. Socialcast
7. Broadcast
Conclusion
Notes
Disclaimer
Contact Niki Faldemolaei
Bonus Material
Biography

A Tiny Snippet of Code Is Changing Everything
Hitting for the Cycle Loop
How Do Advertising Executives Perceive the Value of Attribution?
So How Do You Attribute the Percentage of the Sale Rewarded to
Which Elements of this Funnel?
Why Should Your Team be Using a Multi-Touch Attribution
Model?
Multi-Touch Models in Use Today
Final Analysis
Contact Steven Laurvick
Bonus Material
Biography

The Buyer (or Referrer)
The Learner
Organic Keywords vs. PPC
Keeping an Open Mind for New Keywords

Biographies

MICHAEL ALF

After a global senior executive career, Michael decided to start his own business. He is founder of the Virtual Summit Formula, author of multiple international #1 best-selling books, who also helps clients create and publish books to help them with their positioning in the marketplace.

His specialty is virtual summits that attract hundreds and thousands of participants, grow and elevate a business, and create significant exposure in the marketplace. With summits like Thermie Living Lifestyle Summit, Freedom Business Summit, Ultimate Man Summit, Entrepreneurial Executive Summit or the Healthy Weight Summit, Michael has developed multiple approaches and a wealth of experience around virtual summits.

Before his entrepreneurial journey, Michael was a senior executive with extensive experience in global, regional and local roles in IT leadership, consulting, transformation, business development and general management within the services business. He has had broad exposure to retail, energy, utilities and FMCG, with particular strength in logistics, working across all modes from mail, express, logistics, freight, rail, ports and corporate services (procurement, HR and finance). He started his career with the Federal Armed Forces in Germany attaining the rank of Captain.

IAN BOSLER

Ian Bosler has published three International #1 Bestselling business books and is a serial entrepreneur. After a very successful corporate career in senior marketing and sales roles, he founded Intertype in 2004. Intertype started as a typical printing business but is now helping small, medium and large businesses to unlock profitable growth by improving their marketing and sales communications. He has been involved with the printing industry for over 30 years. From large multinational companies to his own start-up, Ian's printing experience encompasses packaging, business forms, commercial print, mail house, security printing, digital printing, and print management.

During his time at these organizations he worked closely with senior executives of major corporations in Australia, UK, USA, and throughout Asia. This exposed him to the communication processes across most industry sectors including Banking & Finance, Education, Manufacturing, Mining, Insurance, as well as all levels of government.

While there have been many achievements throughout his career, his biggest success has come from his own start-up printing company which he founded in 2004. This business has evolved to provide comprehensive marketing and sales communications products and services to an enviable list of Australian and international clients. By deploying a highly-automated marketing and sales communications approach within his own printing business, it has been recognized by the printing industry heavyweight, Fuji Xerox, as representing the model for the future of the printing industry.

Originally from Mudgee, a small country town in Australia, he now lives with his wife and son in Melbourne. He loves the ocean, is an avid sailor, and enjoys indoor archery.

KAROL CLARK, MSN, RN

Karol Clark, MSN, RN, is a #1 best-selling author and entrepreneur. As the founder and CEO of Weight Loss Practice Builder, Karol helps self-insured corporations implement cost-effective weight loss surgery options (including a comprehensive 12-month follow-up program), and incorporate a successful non-surgical weight loss program (My Weight Loss Academy) into their health plan for their employees so they not only lose weight but understand how to keep it off for life!

Karol and her team also certify on-site corporate physicians or private physician groups to effectively provide individualized counseling to accompany these weight loss programs.

Karol can be reached at:

Karol@WeightLossPracticeBuilder.com

On LinkedIn at:
https://www.linkedin.com/in/clarkarol.
You can also visit her business sites at:
www.CFWLS.com,
www.WeightLossPracticeBuilder.com
www.YourBestSellerBook.com.

JERRY DREESSEN

Jerry Dreessen has been studying and implementing keyword
search and website optimization since 2008. He is constantly learning
the latest techniques and is always testing new and creative ways
to bring clients' content to the "front of the search engine line" to
generate organic as well as paid traffic.

He holds a Certification in Author Expert Marketing Machines,
as well as being CEO of Who Is Your Webguy, a local and national
client-marketing company. He is a master close-up magician, with
three original illusions on the market; and in his spare time sails Hobie
Cats with his wife, Jenny. He is happily married with three kids, and is
not so happily an owner of three cats.

NIKI FALDEMOLAEI

Niki Faldemolaei is the author of three #1 international best-
selling books, and certified marketing technologist and strategist,
Niki helps companies master the digital age so that they can grow and
profit.

Niki served 20 years in corporate biotechnology and new media
industries followed by 10 years in entrepreneurial product and service
launches, campaigns utilizing cutting-edge intelligence and live event
promotions for celebrity athletes and pioneering healers.

While working with the Newspaper Association of America,
IMG Creative and Proelite, Niki achieved successful client placements
in *USA Today, Newsweek, Washington Post, NY Times, Huffington Post,
Muscle & Fitness;* at the Cannes Film Festival and Toronto Film
Festival; as well as on the Sundance Channel, National Geographic
Channel, and Showtime. Niki has also earned agency, publishing and
NY Times interactive awards.

In her spare time she contributes to non-profit charities and was blessed to run a branch church ONAC Indigenous School of Temple Arts. Visit them at http://indigenous-nations.org.

BARRY D. GUMAER, SR., MBA

Barry D. Gumaer, Sr., MBA, Digital Marketing Consultant, Producer, Speaker, Author. Barry is a highly-accomplished specialized marketer, author, speaker, consultant and digital video marketing consultant with highly-skilled proficiencies in marketing, lead generation, customer retentions, and an exceptional technical expertise in audio, video and creative production designs background in corporate meetings, events and entertainment, who brings results to the companies he consults. He has been producing and directing videos since 1967 and uses his expertise to benefit varied enterprises in accomplishing their marketing and performance goals.

A serial entrepreneur since 1977, Barry has established businesses in video production, equipment and services; marketing; entertainment and retail; and web-specific design services.

Throughout a career of more than 40 years, he has worked with more than 350 of the Fortune 500 companies and executives including IBM, Disney, Boeing, Hershey, Sun Microsystems and CBS; past U.S. Presidents and other government officials including U.S. Supreme Court Justices; A-List celebrities; countless associations, medical societies, facilities and non-profit enterprises. He works with local establishments in every conceivable category of business enterprise, specializing in enterprises with revenue of $1 to $15 million, furthering their efforts toward increasing customers, revenues and ROI.

Barry D. Gumaer, Sr., MBA, is the President/CEO of Complete AV, LLC, a marketing solutions consulting company specializing in Video Marketing Solutions, website and Direct Response marketing services and video production. Established in 1983, it is based in Palm Springs, California.

Guiding Statement: "When the student is ready ... the teacher appears!"

JOE (JT) IPPOLITO

Joe (JT) Ippolito is a former executive for IBM, Xerox, AT&T, and NEC, He is the Founder and CEO of Media Marketing Management. As an award-winning entrepreneur, business owner, speaker, author, and consultant, he specializes in cross-channel marketing strategies that help companies increase their revenue with his proprietary tactics.

His websites are located at: http://www.mediamarketingmgmt.com and http://www.jtippolito.com.

Joe has worked on complex technology solutions with C-level executives in boardroom settings. Having received numerous awards, clients have included: Disney, Mattel, Sony, Warner Bros., and Fox.

A self-styled "media disrupter," Joe's ideas challenge the status quo of new media marketing. For 34 years, he's dedicated his career to his unique brand of high-leverage marketing, bringing great success to former employers and dozens of name-brand clients.

MIGUEL DE JESÚS, MBA, CPC

Miguel de Jesús, MBA, CPC (Certified Professional Coach), Executive Coach, Speaker, Author, and Marketing Consultant.

Miguel is a highly-accomplished, results-oriented C-level leader with more than 20 years experience leading business management and global sales/marketing, with two Fortune 500 companies.

A leader in running a $150M sales organization as VP of Sales, hc has most currently been providing leadership and sales training to professionals as a Leadership Consultant and Coach.

He is a digital marketing professional helping business leaders, authors, speakers, coaches and other professionals to improve their marketing efforts to gain more visitors, leads, and client conversions.

As a keynote speaker, and transformational change agent, Miguel brings his insights and wisdom to public and corporate audiences.

His books *Success Leaves Clues* and *So, What Do You Do?* were published on November 15, 2013. http://amzn.to/1ad6e0P

His most recent best-selling book, *Let Your Emotional Intelligence Do The Talking!*, is available in both Kindle and paperback editions on Amazon. http://bit.ly/LetYourEmotionalIntelligence

Guiding Statement: "Struggle is Optional ... Success is a Choice!"

STEVEN LAURVICK

Steven Laurvick is a best-selling author, business owner and marketing consultant. His marketing company has published eight titles in paperback, e-book and audio formats. His first best seller, *Oracular Marketing: How to Build an Evergreen Online Marketing Platform for Your Business, Products and Services,* is a marketing manual for small business start-ups.

As the moderator of the podcasts *The Online Marketing Guy and Caregiver Support,* Steve has interviewed dozens of thought leaders, medical device inventors, manufacturers and business owners. His international #1 best seller, *How the Experts Make More Money in Less Time: In-Depth Interviews with 9 Cross-Channel Marketing Professionals,* is a compilation of the transcripts of the best interviews conducted by Steve on *The Online Marketing Guy* video podcast.

The owner of EnableMobility.com, MedAme.com, WheelchairShowers.com and other online venues with over 3,000 medical products, he is an expert at marketing on Amazon, Facebook, Pinterest, Twitter, Instagram, eBay, Shopify, WooCommerce, Google Merchant and other venues for physical and digital products online.

A certified consultant with over 100 Instant Customer/TPNI Engage client sessions, Steve has helped dozens of entrepreneurs and business owners achieve success by consulting on the use of CRM systems with video marketing, email and SMS text messaging, and setting up automated social media delivery systems.

His company AME LLC is a marketing company that uses retargeted marketing, app creation, video production, webcast production, SEO, affiliate marketing, and PPC promotions.

SHARON MACLEAN

Sharon MacLean, President, WorldGate Media believes we need entrepreneurs and industry leaders to thrive, and flourish, in our linked-up world.

As owner and publisher of a noted business magazine for 21 years, Sharon created content with forward-thinking solutions. An early adopter of social media, she positioned the magazine online using Twitter, Facebook, LinkedIn, and automated email marketing.

Sharon originated the famous "Sizzling Under 30" that celebrated 200 young business leaders, "Women in Business," "Family Business," "International Business," and "Visionaries in Technology," among others. The Canadian entrepreneur later led an investor-backed start-up in its mission to create a marketing portal for wellness experts.

The veteran strategist now helps successful business people adapt their traditional methods to social enterprise.

STEPHEN SABER

Stephen Saber is currently the CEO of The Pulse Network (OTCBB: TPNI). The Pulse Network provides a cloud-based platform focused on content marketing and event solutions. The company helps clients ranging from Fortune 500 companies to small and mid-size companies boost awareness, drive lead generation, and enhance client engagement through content marketing, campaign management and event registration with a social and digital backbone.

Stephen was formerly president of CrossTech Partners and CEO of New Marketing Labs, which merged with The Pulse Network in the spring of 2011. Earlier in his career he was a managing director at Cambridge Technology Partners (CTP) – one of the fastest-growing public IT services companies. CTP became the leading IT consulting and systems integration firm focused on the deployment of client-server based business applications for Fortune 500 clients. Stephen has played a leading advisory role in major M&A transactions ranging from $30M to $450M in Digital Media and IT. Stephen received his M.B.A. from Harvard Business School and B.A. from Harvard University.

OLIVIER G. TAUPIN

Olivier G. Taupin is at the front line of tomorrow's social media: vertical business networks. He also is the architect of the *10-Step Social Media Leadership – The Taupin Model©* which guides CEOs on how to assess, plan, develop, and lead the social influence and the media content of their social media strategy.

For Olivier, expanding a company's social influence is no different than boosting the membership of a community, and he knows about communities: He founded the one-million-member Linked:HR, the largest professional group on LinkedIn worldwide. He also is the inspiration and the process strategist behind more than one hundred large business communities including Linked:Energy with 230K members, Next Dimension Careers with 120K members, and Linked:Seattle with 54K members.

Olivier lives at the foot of Mount Rainier, near Seattle, Washington. He is blessed to have been married for 20 years to his best friend and is the proud father of two highly-creative teenagers.

MELODIE RUSH

Melodie Rush is a trained Statistician and holds a technical MBA. She has presented and consulted with many Fortune 500 companies both domestically and internationally. Being a geek has not always been cool, but it has certainly given her the opportunity to teach and consult on many analytical topics across many industries. Her biggest strength is relating technical information to nontechnical folks.

Melodie has an uncanny ability to simplify topics and chunk them into small bite-size pieces that even those afraid of analytics can understand. Melodie is an experienced speaker both live and virtual via webinars, having led more than 1500 webinars since 2001. She knows what works and what doesn't when it comes to doing presentations.

She is the best-selling author of the book *Deliver Webinars Like a Pro*. Melodie launched "We Create MVPs" to share her knowledge and expertise by helping those new to webinars become powerful, influential presenters. Additionally, Melodie works with her clients to become recognized experts in their chosen niche through video, social media and online marketing.

Her experience includes creating and implementing surveys, analyzing data, coordinating presentations from one hour to three days. Melodie lives in Colorado with her husband and two cats. She loves to travel, scrapbook, and play with technology. In her spare time, she volunteers at the Denver Zoo as a Docent.

PAT ZIEMER

Pat Ziemer is the owner of Magna Wave. The company's therapy devices are used extensively on racehorses, performance horses, and professional athletes. Five recent Kentucky Derby winners and numerous world champions in many horse disciplines utilize the therapy regularly.

In 2007, Pat acquired the rights to the PEMF device, repackaged it, branded it as Magna Wave and hit the road marketing the Magna Wave brand. Since 2007 Pat has placed over 600 Magna Wave devices into the market for private and professional use, primarily in the equine marketplace. The company is now moving into the areas of human and small animal therapy.

Chapter 1: How Healthy Is Your Corporation?

5 Steps to Lowering Your Healthcare Costs While Improving Employee Productivity, Employee Retention and Enhancing Your Customer Experience

by Karol H. Clark, MSN, RN

The health of any corporation can be defined and measured in many different ways. Is it your financial bottom line or the aggregate cost of healthcare premiums for your employees? Is it the environment and culture of your corporation? Or could it be your retention rate, your customer satisfaction rate, your absenteeism rate or your safety rating?

Finally, could it be the overall perceived corporate wellness attitude conveyed from your board of directors to your leadership team (including you) all the way down to your lowest wage earner? The truth is none of these answers are incorrect.

Every metric mentioned is very important to the overall health of your corporation. However, there is one factor that influences them all – a critical factor that will make or break not only the health of your organization, but your ability to survive (and ultimately thrive). This factor is the individual health of every single member of your team which, when combined, becomes the overall health (and energy) of your corporation.

Numerous articles and business books validate the fact that your employees are one of your greatest assets, especially those that are truly engaged and talented (1). *"Not only are your employees a great asset, but one that will give your company its competitive advantage."* It's no wonder why attracting and retaining excellent employees is one of the top issues keeping today's CEOs awake at night (2, 3), as well as why focusing on your people is a critical business strategy discussed in so many top corporate business books such as *Good to Great (4), Firms of Endearment (5), The Advantage (6), The Breakthrough Company (7),* and many more.

The purpose of this chapter is to help you determine not only the status of the overall health of your corporation, but how to create healthy changes that will significantly influence nearly every important aspect of your company – particularly the areas of employee productivity, employee retention, and ultimately enhancing your overall customer experience. This will position you for significant growth … and fun! Does this sound too good to be true? I challenge you to read on, open your mind to the possibilities, commit to creating your "healthier" corporation, and then reap the many benefits.

Why Five Steps?

Well, because five is a reasonable number. Seriously, there is no need to complicate improving the health of your corporation beginning with the individual health and happiness of you and your employees. It's a win/win situation.

While there are a number of hurdles such as the current state of the healthcare industry today, the rising rate of obesity, and the clear inability to force individuals to make better choices, there are viable options that create great results.

Your employees need to have them available and be motivated to ACTIVELY participate. This will benefit your corporation. Notice, I do not say your employees deserve to have them available with no skin in the game. In my 23+ years of experience, this rarely works.

Below are the Five Steps to Improved Corporate Health:
1. Understand Today's Healthcare Environment
2. Choose to Thrive Instead of Survive
3. Review Your Options

4.   Challenge Yourself, Consider Something New, and Act with Purpose

5.   Measure Your ROI (in more ways than one)

Added Bonus: Take the "How Healthy Is Your Corporation?" Quiz (www.healthycorpquiz.com).

Step 1: Understand Today's Healthcare Environment

I might be aging myself but my twin sister and I were born in 1963. We were the last of six children born in Ohio to parents who survived the Depression and worked very hard to provide for all of us. We lived in a house they contracted/built themselves, had balanced meals on the table, a good education, and the opportunity to go to college. One of my older sisters had medical problems and about 15 surgeries in her first 18 years of life.

My father worked at NASA and had other entrepreneurial endeavors in order to provide for what we needed. He (and my mother) taught me that hard work pays off and that you can accomplish anything you set your mind to! I only wish they had been able to play as hard as they worked. I am grateful to them and my large family. Fortunately, healthcare was pretty much a guarantee with full-time employment at that time ... and a lot less complicated.

I always knew I wanted to be a nurse. I was a candy-striper at the local hospital and went to Kent State University for my nursing degree. I have always been very driven. Within one year after starting my nursing career, I was promoted to Nurse Manager, began earning my graduate degree, and focusing on a career in hospital administration. Things were still great – healthcare was a benefit we took for granted; and we even had the luxury of 100% tuition reimbursement!

Fast forward to today. Although I vowed I never would get mixed up (aka fall in love) with a resident at the hospital I worked, that's exactly what happened. Thus, I am married to one of the most experienced and yet humble bariatric surgeons in the United States

(Dr. Thomas W. Clark) and, believe it or not, we actually work very well together.

Tom has always been ahead of his time (which is exciting and scary all at the same time) with his forward-thinking ideas, and I am the "go-to gal" helping to bring our dreams to fruition through teamwork, creativity and building effective systems. This has afforded us (and our team) the opportunity to provide "out of the box" concierge-style services that have significantly improved the health of well over 6,000 people in and around Virginia where we live.

We attract patients from as far away as Africa as well. The model we have created for integrated comprehensive surgical and non-surgical weight loss, nutrition and fitness services years ago is finally becoming more of the norm, and our model has been successfully duplicated.

While Tom continues to focus on patient care, speaking and education, I now take our turn-key systems and integrate them into corporations and primary care physicians' offices. It's an abundance mindset that affords us the ability to reach beyond our local communities; and being able to help many more people is extremely rewarding.

We work hard (just like our parents) but we try to take time to play hard as well (a balance I know you understand is not easy). The health and well-being of our team is paramount and significantly impacts our near-zero staff turnover rate, off-the-charts patient satisfaction, and self-directed staff that aren't afraid to speak up when a process/product can be improved upon for the benefit of our patients and/or our organization.

We are very far from perfect but we strive for health, balance, and improvement each and every day. For optimal success, we believe you need to surround yourself with the best people and lead the health of your organization.

As you know, the healthcare environment changes over the past 20 years have been astounding, particularly since the inception of the Affordable Care Act (the landmark U.S. health insurance legislation know as Obamacare) that was passed in 2010. Today there is still uncertainty regarding its long-term effects, and a majority of Americans don't feel good about their healthcare.

A major reason for this is the fact that many middle-income Americans are watching the cost of health coverage rise faster than their median incomes. Thus, obtaining healthcare coverage does not necessarily correlate to the ability to pay for it.

As a large (or small) employer, you are feeling the pinch as well and facing tough decisions. With nearly two-thirds of Americans having employer-sponsored health insurance (approximately 171 million people), the burden of complying with the Affordable Care Act falls on businesses of all sizes **(8)**. While you want to continue to offer an employer-sponsored health program viewed as the typical "gold standard" for attracting talented employees, you may begin (if you haven't already) to feel it is becoming quite a burden.

It varies by state, but due to significant jumps in premiums as a result of provisions in the health-care law, some corporations are considering tactics such as increasing employee cost-sharing, reducing the overall number of full-time employees, delaying hiring, and reducing employee hours. You see this more often in smaller companies but these trends continue.

Unfortunately, while sometimes necessary, these actions are not conducive to creating a growth-minded environment and the ability to attract ideal employee candidates. While you must consider all of the legal coverage requirements, how taxes and fees will affect you, and whether or not you can provide coverage, you must take a step back and analyze what is in concert with your overall culture and corporate goals. A knee-jerk reaction is rarely the right decision and just following the crowd may work short term but will likely compromise your values in the long run.

Step 2: Choose to Thrive Instead of Survive

I am not an attorney, I am not an accountant, I am not an insurance specialist, and I am not an economist. I am not telling you what to do. That is not my place. I am here as an advocate for optimal personal and corporate health with quality, results-oriented wellness options. I am also here to encourage you to challenge the status quo and do your due diligence.

Utilize your brilliant team to evaluate your options and base your decision on not only your financial situation, but what supports the health of your organization. Complete your research and be true to your values. Healthcare coverage decisions are for you and your governing board of directors to make together.

The 2018 excise tax is drawing near. Thus it is imperative to examine your business risk and determine whether or not your platform adheres to requirements. Consideration needs to be made as to the best way to manage costs, how best to involve your employees, incorporate the latest technology for engagement, realize the highest-quality outcomes, and how to best improve the overall health of your employees and ultimately your corporation.

Whatever your decision, you will be ahead of the game (and in better compliance) if your workforce is as healthy as possible (emotionally and physically). This means that you must support your employees and provide them with the tools they need to improve their health. Like your organization, they need to thrive, not just survive.

You cannot control their actions but you can provide them with a culture, environment, motivation, outcome-oriented programs, and role models so they not only can and want to make positive changes, but are expected to as well. Then you will be best positioned to realize the corporate benefits that come from having employees functioning at their optimal level of health.

Step 3: Review Your Options

The rules for the Affordable Care Act vary depending upon the size of your organization. If you determine that according to current strict regulatory rules you have fewer than 50 employees you can choose whether or not you want to provide insurance for employees. You can purchase insurance through the Small Business Health Options Program (SHOP). You can learn more at www.HealthCare. gov.

Another option (one I utilize for our corporation) is to work through your options and requirements with a qualified insurance broker. He/she can review your best options for a full-insured health plan and/or combination plans to best meet the needs of your particular organization. I have found our agent to be a wealth of information and willing to review all options and assist with compliance so as to avoid unnecessary fees or penalties.

For larger corporations (50+ full-time employees), The Affordable Care Act includes an employer mandate designed to force firms to provide full-time employees with comprehensive health insurance. Employers are also required to limit the amount of premiums some employees pay as a percentage of their wage income (or pay the consequences). Corporations employing 50-99 full-time workers have until 2016 to comply (8).

For large corporations, another common option is to have a self-insured (self-funded) health plan instead of the traditional full-insured health plan. Larger corporations often add a stop-loss or excess-loss insurance policy to limit their risk for catastrophic events or claims that significantly exceed what is expected for aggregate (group of covered persons) coverage. *"Self-funding empowers employers with the ability to customize a health plan to meet the specific needs of their workforce without compromising access to quality medical and company profit margins"* (9).

In addition to traditional full-insured health plans and self-insured health plans, larger corporations may choose to provide a modification to the self-insured health plan option. These include a partially self-insured plan with an integrated Health Reimbursement Arrangement (HRA) or a self-insured medical reimbursement plan such as a Healthcare Reimbursement Plan (HRP) (10). The HRP is not actually health insurance but a plan that provides reimbursement for eligible health insurance premium instead of offering a group health plan (10).

There is a lot to consider. All options carry risks and benefits. However, you will find self-funded programs are becoming more common and a preferable choice for larger corporations.

Step 4: Challenge Yourself, Consider Something New, and Act with Purpose

So how can you help your employees and your corporation become healthier with as little cost as possible and potentially save money too? I will share a number of ideas that will help your employees (your corporation) become healthier. If your employees are healthy, these options help them maintain their good health.

If they are overweight, these options not only help them lose weight but also increase their lean body mass (more muscle = higher metabolism). Everyone learns how to control the hormones that can make them act somewhat out of whack (and often grumpy/tired/unproductive) and become more engaged in an environment they enjoy. Believe me; simply adding fruit choices to meetings, break rooms and cafeterias is not the answer.

Understand that every corporation is different. The key is to look at the aggregate health of your employees and look where you can do the most good and cause no harm. For example, if you have a primarily healthy organization, you may want to focus your efforts on actions such as the following:

- Make environmental changes to your break room (making it more inviting to distract people from eating at their desks or going out for fast food).

- Begin an interactive newsletter and/or private social media "healthy" communication hub. Make it interesting and fun with graphics, videos, "now I can" success stories, infographics, podcasts and upbeat stories.

- Create a corporate private online membership site for education, webinars, podcasts, kudos announcements, and more!

- Build a simple, corporate-specific health app that tracks a variety of health parameters such as weight, macronutrient intake (especially total protein, carbohydrate and calories/day), and BMI. We do this with an interactive scale so we can track success easier and provide feedback for positive results and to catch trends before they become a problem. Creating an app is easier than you think and fun to implement/promote.

- Offer a "workout at your desk" online video series. We offer this and it is amazing the fitness that can be accomplished with just you and your office chair for 10 minutes. As an added benefit, the mental break generally results in higher productivity and creativity.

•   Eliminate candy at your work area. Did you know that *"People who have candy in or on their desk reported weighing 15.4 pounds more than those who didn't"?* (11)

•   Download a free, customizable *12-Step Guide to Weight Loss Success* from www.HealthyCorpQuiz.com. Make it your own with your logo and distribute it to everyone at your corporation. It has opened eyes and changed lives.

•   Have a 4-week or 6-week challenge. Partner your employees and watch them do a friendly competition for things like total grams of protein, controlled carbohydrate intake, total number of steps, percentage of weight lost, change in BMI, and more! Keep it to a reasonable time frame and don't make the measurement too difficult to measure and record. Add it into your app for ease of tracking.

•   Offer rewards – they don't have to be monetary. However, working this into your wellness program (i.e., discounts on health insurance premiums) can help you meet the requirements for the Affordable Care Act.

•   Don't forget to address your employee's financial health as well. Helping them maneuver money management and retirement planning is also helpful with long-term retention and respect for an employer that truly cares about them and their situation.

•   Just to mention a few.… If your programs aren't engaging, they won't likely be very successful. To address those employees with more significant health problems including but not limited to obesity (BMI > 30), morbid obesity (BMI > 40) and chronic diseases, you can incorporate the strategies listed above. However, you will need to add additional programs that can still be of minimal cost with a maximum return.

Especially if you are self-insured, such strategies can include:

•   Partnering with physician(s) in your area that demonstrate outstanding outcomes when it comes to working with employees with health problems. They should be board-certified as well as part of a certified center of excellence as appropriate. A local or employed physician is often more trusted and may result in a higher level of employee engagement.

• Beginning a true medical weight loss program with proven results. An example is our online interactive and comprehensive weight loss program called My Weight Loss Academy™ that focuses on personal nutrition, behavior and fitness. You can offer this program to your employees as an independent program, or your on-site practitioners can be certified to provide individualized counseling to accompany the program. There is no reason to reinvent the wheel since the comprehensive curriculum is easy to implement and your practitioners are given the training/tools they need for optimal implementation.

• Consider partnering with health systems or Centers of Excellence and package pricing for many surgical procedures and health services instead of following the traditional (generally more costly) insurance route. Some companies turn to medical tourism for this; but in many cases, package prices offered here in the United States can be even more affordable than traveling to another country.

For example, as shown on ABC News (12), a progressive and forward-thinking North Carolina-based company shared that they have saved their self-insured company about $10 million in healthcare over five years by sending their employees abroad for surgeries such as joint replacements and weight loss surgery. In fact, the employees receive money (instead of paying co-pays) for choosing this option.

While outcomes were shown to be positive and the employees were grateful and satisfied, the same sleeve gastrectomy procedure that cost the company nearly $20,000 overseas could have been done in Virginia for just under $14,000 at the Center for Weight Loss Success and includes a full one-year follow-up program by one of the most experienced bariatric surgeons in the U.S. at an outstanding Center of Excellence facility.

Negotiating package pricing in the United States for life-saving procedures such as this can save self-insured corporations millions of dollars. It is definitely something to seriously consider and a win-win for the company and employee.

If you already have a wellness program with excellent outcomes, I applaud you. You are making a positive impact on your employees and your corporation. If you do not have such options in place, I ask you to consider some of the options presented here (which are certainly not all-inclusive). I ask you not only to consider them but to take action. There is no time like the present! Don't forget to take your corporate health quiz at www.HealthyCorpQuiz.com.

Step 5: Measure Your ROI (in more ways than one)

The Affordable Care Act offers financial incentives to encourage employer wellness programs, such as reimbursement for the cost of fitness center membership, on-site fitness classes, weight loss or nutrition programs and smoking cessation programs. These incentives apply to wellness programs already in effect as well as new ones as long as they meet specific criteria. Thus, not only will implementing a wellness program promote a healthy work environment, but it also can result in a true return on investment (ROI).

While I am here to present more than just wellness programs, I must share that *"Wellness programs don't just benefit employees – they benefit companies too. Specifically, they reduce the productivity losses resulting from employee or family health problems which, according to the CDC, cost them $1,685 per employee, per year. Healthy employees have fewer absences. It stands to reason that they are also more engaged, energetic and enthusiastic – all of which translate to higher performance"* (13), not to mention fewer physician visits and overall health costs.

In summary, your imagination is the only limitation when it comes to creating ways to improve the health of yourself and your employees. Weight is a natural area to focus on because it permeates every aspect of health; and the disease "obesity" is at the root of so many illnesses such as diabetes, hypertension, sleep apnea, metabolic syndrome, degenerative joint disease, some cancers, fatigue, mobility issues, and so much more. If you correct obesity, most of these other diseases significantly improve or resolve completely. Weight loss also improves your overall positivity, performance, self-esteem and level of energy.

We have experienced results that exceed national averages with thousands of people. You see, once they understand the basics of weight loss, including how to easily control your hormones that cause weight gain such as ghrelin, insulin and leptin to name a few, a light bulb often goes off and people realize that they have been making weight loss far too difficult. For some, affordable weight loss surgery with a comprehensive follow-up behavior modification program may be the best answer.

No matter what, it is a partnership that reaps benefits that aren't always measurable by a laboratory number or test. Your partnership to help your employees lose weight allows them to participate in activities with their family and at work, exercise without pain, fit in (in more ways than one), and live their life to the fullest.

This happiness permeates their home relationships and their work performance. It is amazing to watch people blossom as their weight comes off. You see, life is what you do minute-to-minute and day-to-day. Being able to enjoy all life has to offer is one of the best things you can do for yourself and for your employees. Help them tend to their health and they will usually be grateful forever.

Thus, employee productivity improves, they feel a bond and are more likely to stay with your organization, and their happiness permeates their customer service skills. The investment you both make pays great dividends and you both will reap the benefits of a job well done.

Don't forget to check out the health of your organization and gain access to free customizable healthy employee tools at www. HealthyCorpQuiz.com.

Notes

(1)   http://www.gallup.com/businessjournal/298/people-arent-your-greatest-asset.aspx. Accessed September 2015.

(2)   http://americasmarkets.usatoday.com/2015/04/27/ceos-tell-all-what-keeps-them-up-at-night/. Accessed September 2015.

(3)   https://hbr.org/2015/03/the-3-things-ceos-worry-about-the-most. Accessed September 2015.

(4)   Collins, J. (2001). Good to great: *Why some companies make the leap...and others don't.* New York, NY: Harper Business.

(5)   Sisodia, R., Wolfe, D., Sheth, J. (2014). *Firms of Endearment: How world-class companies profit from passion and purpose.* Upper Saddle River, New Jersey: Pearson Education.

(6)   Lencioni, P. (2012). *The advantage: Why organizational health trumps everything else in business.* San Francisco, CA: Jossey-Bass.

(7)   McFarland, K.R. (2008). *The Breakthrough Company: How everyday companies become extraordinary performers.* New York, NY: Random House.

(8)   Herrick, M.D. "The effects of the Affordable Care Act on small business"; National Center for Policy Analysis; No. 356; June 12, 2014; http://www.ncpa.org/pub/st356. Accessed September 2015.

(9)   Edelheit, J. (2014). "Self-funding: Passport to Medical Tourism for US Employers." Medical Tourism Association White Paper. (http://www.medicaltourismassociation.com/upload/upload_SELF%20FUNDED%20WHITEPAPER.pdf). Accessed September 2015.

(10)   Moss, M. (2014). Fully-Insured vs. Self-Insured (Self-Funded) health plans. http://www.zanebenefits.com/blog/fully-insured-vs-self-insured-self-funded-health-plans.

(11)   Wansink, B. (2014). *Slim by design: Mindless eating solutions for everyday life.* New York, NY: William Morrow.

(12)   http://abcnews.go.com/Health/americans-surgeries-overseas-us-companies-medical-tourism-health/story?id=20423011. Accessed September 2015.

(13)   Moran, Brian (2014). http://www.medicaltourismmag.com/power-one-little-thing-thinking-small-secret-meeting-corporate-wellness-goals/. Accessed September 2014.

Contact Karol Clark

Karol@CFWLS.com
https://www.linkedin.com/in/clarkarol
www.CFWLS.com
www.WeightLossPracticeBuilder.com
www.YourBestSellerBook.com

Bonus Material

Verify the health of your organization and gain access to free customizable healthy employee tools at www.HealthyCorpQuiz.com.

Biography

Karol Clark, MSN, RN, is a #1 best-selling author and entrepreneur. As the founder and CEO of Weight Loss Practice Builder, Karol helps self-insured corporations implement cost-effective weight loss surgery options (including a comprehensive 12-month follow-up program), and incorporate a successful non-surgical weight loss program (My Weight Loss Academy) into their health plan for their employees so they not only lose weight but understand how to keep it off for life!

Karol and her team also certify on-site corporate physicians or private physician groups to effectively provide individualized counseling to accompany these weight loss programs.

Karol can be reached at:
Karol@WeightLossPracticeBuilder.com
On LinkedIn at https://www.linkedin.com/in/clarkkarol

You can also visit her business sites at: www.CFWLS.com, www. WeightLossPracticeBuilder.com, and www.YourBestSellerBook.com.

Chapter 2: Emotional Intelligence

90% of Top Performers Have High EQ. Are You One of Them?
by Miguel A. de Jesús

Emotional intelligence (EQ) is the ability to use emotions effectively. Since the publication of the initial research in 1990, innovative organizations have begun testing how to integrate EQ into training and hiring to gain competitive advantage. It is becoming increasingly clear that these skills are the foundation of high-performing organizations.

A range of implementation strategies have been used to deploy EQ, primarily in selection and development. The competencies are measurable and learnable; they can be improved through training and coaching. The most effective implementation strategies seek to integrate EQ into the organizational culture.

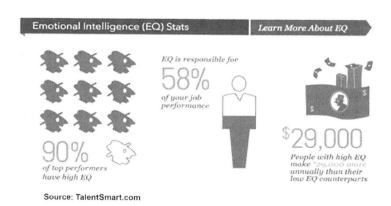

Source: TalentSmart.com

29

While there are numerous implementation strategies, researched EQ applications include:

• increased sales performance through recruiting and training more emotionally-intelligent salespeople.

• improved customer service through recruiting higher EQ customer service reps.

• superior leadership performance by developing and recruiting for executive EQ. Companies have demonstrated that using EQ in training and organizational climate change can reduce costs associated with turnover, absenteeism, and low performance. Research has provided clear evidence that emotionally-intelligent leaders are more successful.

Many of these studies yield bottom-line results. At PepsiCo, for example, executives selected for EQ competencies generated 10% more productivity. High EQ salespeople at L'Oréal brought in $2.5 million more in sales. An EQ initiative at Sheraton helped increase market share by 24%. The U.S. Air Force is using EQ to screen pararescue jumpers to save $190 million.

One of the most important applications of EQ is in helping leaders foster a workplace climate conducive to high performance. These workplaces yield significantly higher productivity, retention, and profitability; and emotional intelligence appears key to this competitive advantage.

What Keeps CEOs Awake at Night?

As a CEO you have an incredible level of pressure to perform, to keep the business making money, and to make the right decisions to not only maintain the status quo but to create the conditions that allow the business to expand and grow.

Leadership at this level is not for the faint of heart, but it is very normal and natural for anyone to fall into the trap of second-guessing decisions, trying to read tea leaves in the bottom of the cup, and trying to harness trends to their advantage. The problem is that this type of constant reflection not only keeps you up at night, but it restricts your ability to be an effective decision maker in the now and in future.

Accepting the Issues

One of the most essential elements or skills to develop as a CEO is to accept the issues that are causing the distress and worry and find a way to work through them. A professional in the field of business development, sales management, and leadership who is also a business or executive coach is a great resource.

The biggest issues that keep business owners and SEOs awake at night include:

• **Attracting and Retaining Employees** – Talent management, or the ability to keep your top employees and to avoid bringing less-qualified and skilled employees onboard, is a critical concern. Most business leaders understand their employees are their company, and they have the ability to make or break any business at any level.

• **Regulations** – Regulatory issues may be impossible to control, but that doesn't mean they aren't something to worry about. Talking to an executive coach and developing a structured approach to handling these situations and accessing resources allows you to accommodate new and ever-changing regulations.

• **Global Competition** – The more that globalization occurs, the more competition grows. No longer does a CEO have to know what the company down the road or in another state is doing. He or she has to worry about what a company on the other side of the globe may be able to offer.

The reality is that fear and worry is not a productive use of your mental energy or your resources. By working with an executive coach, any CEO can learn to identify fears, or nagging worries, and develop a plan to address these issues in a positive, productive, and effective way.

Emotional Intelligence

What it is and how you can apply this to your leadership and communication skills, in business and in life.

Studies have revealed that Emotional Intelligence has a significant impact on the success of school children and employees in different settings. This proves how superior EI is to an IQ. Or rather, how EI helps shape the IQ of a more holistic individual who excels at academic and performance leadership at work. I teach others about EI, what their EI is, and how it can change the way they interact with others to produce the desired results.

There are four categories of development required to develop mastery skills in the area of Emotional Intelligence. It is a continuous improvement process. Those areas are: Self-Awareness, Self-Management, Social Awareness, and Relationship Management.

How We Retain Information

Getting a new idea is one thing, but what you do with it once you have it is just as important as getting it in the first place. According to Edgar Dale, his research and development of *Cone of Learning* shows that you remember:

- **10%** of what you read
- **20%** of what you hear
- **30%** of what you see
- **50%** of what you see and hear, and up to
- **90%** of what you see, hear and do

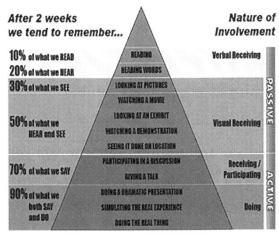

Cone of Learning (Edgar Dale)

After 2 weeks we tend to remember...

Nature of Involvement

10% of what we READ	READING	Verbal Receiving
20% of what we HEAR	HEARING WORDS	
30% of what we SEE	LOOKING AT PICTURES	
	WATCHING A MOVIE	
50% of what we HEAR and SEE	LOOKING AT AN EXHIBIT	Visual Receiving
	WATCHING A DEMONSTRATION	
	SEEING IT DONE ON LOCATION	
70% of what we SAY	PARTICIPATING IN A DISCUSSION	Receiving / Participating
	GIVING A TALK	
90% of what we both SAY and DO	DOING A DRAMATIC PRESENTATION	Doing
	SIMULATING THE REAL EXPERIENCE	
	DOING THE REAL THING	

(PASSIVE / ACTIVE)

Edgar Dale, Audio-Visual Methods in Technology, Holt, Rinehart and Winston.

In their book *The Knowing-Doing Gap*, authors Jeffrey Pfeffer and Robert L. Sutton mention that every year there are 1,700 new business books published, $60 billion spent on training, $43 billion spent on consultants, and our universities turn out 80,000 graduates with MBAs. Yet, most businesses continue to operate day in and day out in much the same ways they have always done.

You see, knowledge without action is no better than no knowledge at all. Just knowing isn't enough. You've got to do something with what you know.

The ideas presented in this chapter and book work. They're not theory. They're not speculation on what "should" work. And they're not philosophical musings. These ideas, concepts and techniques are currently in use by business owners across the country in one form or another. They're being proven in actual field use day in and day out.

They work for others, and they can work for you. But, you're going to have to take the time to study them, understand them, and make the necessary modifications to tailor them to your own personal and business style and operation. And then finally, you're going to have to apply them in your business. So let's take a look at the next question.

How to Train Your EQ Brain

You know emotional intelligence matters, and you've begun to practice. Now you need to learn how to tackle the barriers to self-awareness, self-management, social awareness and managing relationships.

Self-Awareness: Achieve a deeper awareness of your emotions by leaning into the discomfort of those that get in your way. How well do you understand yourself under stress?

Self-Management: Knowing you should self-manage is easier than doing it well. Take control of the key driver of words and actions you later regret – your self-talk.

Social Awareness: Mastering the art of social awareness comes from analyzing what the people and situations in your work life that matter most have to offer you.

Relationship Management: When conflict ensues, the emotions that emerge before, during and after the conflict are what people fear most. It turns out there is a whole host of EQ strategies that can help you.

Anyone who gives ongoing attention to practicing their EQ skills will increase their self-knowledge and ability to handle stress, communicate effectively, make good decisions, manage conflict, be a team player, respond flexibly to change, influence others, and provide top-notch performance.

Companies and individuals have demonstrated that using Emotional Intelligence (EQ) in training and organizational climate change can reduce costs associated with turnover, absenteeism, and low performance. Research has provided clear evidence that emotionally-intelligent leaders are more successful.

Many of these studies yield bottom-line results: At PepsiCo, for example, executives selected for EQ competencies generated 10% more productivity. High EQ salespeople at L'Oréal brought in $2.5 million more in sales. An EQ initiative at Sheraton helped increase market share by 24%. The U.S. Air Force is using EQ to screen pararescue jumpers to save $190 million.

One of the most important applications of EQ is in helping leaders foster a workplace climate conducive to high performance. These workplaces yield significantly-higher productivity, retention, and profitability; and emotional intelligence appears key to this competitive advantage.

The evidence is increasingly compelling. The measurable, learnable skills of emotional intelligence make a significant impact on organizational performance.

EQ may be essential to differentiating world-class organizations in an increasingly-complex and competitive marketplace.

I am often asked about the skills that are required to develop EI, and here I will list three **Self-Awareness Strategies** that you can engage in to make developmental improvements:

1.   Quit treating your feelings as "good" or "bad." Notice your feelings, and don't judge them as good or bad. Remind yourself that they are there to help you understand something important.

2.   Lean into your discomfort. Lean into the discomfort of your moods to explore what they are trying to tell you. To better understand them, notice your physical discomfort, when it happens, and how long it lasts.

3.   Keep a journal about your emotions. At the end of the day for a month, record the feelings that affect you the most (good or bad). After 30 days, read what you captured and underline any triggers and repeated patterns.

My Story

My story and evolution to the study of Emotional Intelligence begins in New York City, New York.

I was born in an East Harlem neighborhood in New York City and then, at the age of four, we moved to the projects. We lived in a large apartment complex comprised of 16 buildings, 14 stories, and eight apartments per floor which all housed a family of three or more. This calculates to approximately 1,664 people residing in a small city block, or in other words, the projects.

Growing up surrounded by that many people and being exposed to diverse ethnicities, religions, and cultures helped me learn how to be respectful, tolerant, and receptive to a variety of ideas and concepts. I learned valuable life lessons growing up in the projects. I developed self-awareness, self-management, social awareness, and relationship management skills through my interactions and observations.

Unfortunately, there was not much training or education available on these subjects, nor thought leaders capable or desirous of making a difference by communicating these new insights and personal development models to us at the time. Through my self-taught skills, I was able to objectively perceive my environment; and at a young age I knew I had to start making my way out of the projects.

I was fortunate to attend and graduate from the High School of Music and Art, a special school for the musically gifted, which was a two-hour roundtrip commute through the NYC subway system. I subsequently enrolled at Long Island University, Brooklyn Campus. Upon graduating with a BS in political science, I chose to pursue an MBA at Columbia University. I left the MBA program before completing my final year and entered the business world because of one thing: money.

My need to earn money far outweighed the benefits of earning an advanced degree. It was time to recalibrate my goals and focus. I buried myself, knee-deep, in the "business of business" by working for Xerox Corporation in a variety of leadership, results-driven roles in both sales and operations for more than 19 years in four different markets. At the time, Xerox was a $15B Fortune 50 company.

After nearly 20 years I decided to shift gears. I have always been entrepreneurially driven and so I decided to take my skills and expertise to a smaller company. I joined the team at Paychex Inc., a $40M Rochester, NY-based payroll and HR company at the time. My direction and leadership significantly contributed to the company's $2B growth.

I held a variety of senior level executive positions, including VP of Sales for the Western U.S., in which I was responsible for the growth and development of 850 Direct Sales Representatives, 130 First Level Managers, and seven Senior Level Regional Sales Managers. My team consistently increased company revenue and market-share growth during my tenure with Paychex. They were a great group of people with a passion for winning and making a difference.

Throughout my life and career I've been curious, fascinated with the dynamics behind how people interact and treat each other. Why are certain people more likable than others? Why do some people manage to get more done? What makes people tick? I became driven to research the reasons why some leaders and individual contributors are more successful securing cooperation and support within their companies than others who seem to become derailed by their inability to gain support and enthusiasm for their ideas and direction.

It all comes down to this: People will work harder and produce more for those whom they know, like, trust, and respect.

This observation and principle applies everywhere — from the basketball court to the boardroom. Regardless of the environment, industry, or company size, it just works. In my quest and thirst to help businesses grow through strong management, I have learned, developed, honed in on, and discovered that the likability factor and the ability to influence stem from the core values and beliefs we hold.

Below are nine core values and beliefs that can positively impact your thought processes and decisions as a Leader:

1. **Compassion:** A deep awareness of and sympathy for another's suffering.

2. **Help Others:** Help other people attain their goals, and offer care and support.

3. **Competence:** Demonstrate a high degree of proficiency and knowledge through above-average effectiveness and efficiency when completing tasks.

4. **Achievement:** Maintain a sense of accomplishment, mastery, and goal achievement.

5. **Loyalty:** Faithfulness, duty, dedication.

6. **Knowledge:** The pursuit of continual learning and development of skills and expertise.

7. **Influence:** Impact and affect the attitudes or opinions of other people: *the power of persuasion.*

8. **Personal Development:** Dedication to maximizing one's potential through self-development.

9. **Coaches and Mentors:** Continually work with highly-qualified coaches and/or mentors whose guidance significantly impacts the choices and decisions you make. The road to success is made easier through associations with the right people at the right time.

Learning, studying, and applying these core values and decisions helped me become the successful businessman I am today. My experiences, the people I have met, and the entire journey have all shaped and molded me into the person I am. Further research led me to an area of expertise: teaching others about Emotional Intelligence (EI) and how it can be more important than an IQ in the business and family setting.

Contact Miguel de Jesús

http://www.linkedin.com/in/migueldj
http://www.coachmiguel.com
http://www.22s.com/34106
https://www.facebook.com/askcoachmiguel
http://http://instantcustomerconnections.com

Bonus Material

Get My Free eBook *Let Your Emotional Intelligence Do The Talking! The 17 Skills Necessary to Influence Your Boss, Family, Team, or Clients for Improved Results*

https://coachmiguel.leadpages.co/ebook/

Biography

Miguel de Jesús, MBA, CPC (Certified Professional Coach), Executive Coach, Speaker, Author, and Marketing Consultant

Miguel is a highly-accomplished, results-oriented C-level leader with more than 20 years experience leading business management and global sales/marketing, with two Fortune 500 companies.

A leader in running a $150M sales organization as VP of Sales, he has most currently ben providing leadership and sales training to professionals as a Leadership Consultant and Coach.

He is a digital marketing professional helping business leaders, authors, speakers, coaches and other professionals to improve their marketing efforts to gain more visitors, leads, and client conversions.

As a keynote speaker, and transformational change agent, Miguel brings his insights and wisdom to public and corporate audiences.

His books *Success Leaves Clues* and *So, What Do You Do?* were published on November 15, 2013. http://amzn.to/1ad6e0P

His most recent best-selling book, *Let Your Emotional Intelligence Do The Talking!*, is available in both Kindle and paperback editions on Amazon. http://bit.ly/LetYourEmotionalIntelligence

Guiding Statement
"Struggle is Optional ... Success is a Choice!"

Chapter 3: It's the Reputation of Your Company!!!

by Joe (JT) Ippolito

"It takes 20 years to build a reputation and five minutes to ruin it. If you think about that you'll do things differently." – **Warren Buffett, Chairman and CEO, Berkshire Hathaway**

Building, protecting and maintaining reputation is undeniably the most important responsibility of today's senior executives. The pace of technology and business change has profoundly altered the role of senior leadership and what is expected of them. Transparency has taken on a new meaning – and level of importance.

Following scandals at Enron, WorldCom and others, corporate governance became political, resulting in an increase in government regulation and changing executive oversight. Sarbanes-Oxley went into effect to reform public accounting and protect investors.

The government stepped in again after the financial meltdown of 2008, leading to bailouts of several automotive and financial companies. These actions led to the Wall Street Reform and Consumer Protection Action of 2010, better known as Dodd-Frank, providing the most significant changes to financial regulation in the United States since the Great Depression.

These business scandals and the economic crises have resulted in a growing mistrust of capitalism and business. According to an annual

Gallup poll, business executives have for the past five years been rated among the lowest professions for honesty and ethical standards.

The advancement of technology, especially social media and mobile devices, compounds reputational pressures for senior executives. Information from multiple sources and media channels is now available 24/7/365. The world has become smaller – yet more complex. These business realities have not gone unnoticed by senior leaders.

Although organizations are seemingly gaining a greater understanding of the importance of reputation and its value, most continue to struggle with identifying the risks and developing strategies to mitigate them.

Today, we live in the "Reputation Economy," a world where who you are as an organization matters as much – and possibly more – to consumers than what you sell. According to a study conducted in June 2012 by the Reputation Institute, 60 percent of the public's willingness to buy, recommend, work for, or invest is driven by their perception of an organization and the values it represents. Yet, few organizations can clearly articulate or meet that challenge.

Too often reputation management is characterized as crisis management. These are not one and the same. Reputation rests at the intersection of three key areas of business strategy and governance that build trust when aligned:

1.   Responsible Business Operations translate into minimal negative impact and maximum positive impact. This includes areas such as environmental, health and safety, and human rights.

2.   Positive Social Impact ensures that a company's expertise and assets address social issues and support social well-being that engages the organization's communities.

3.   Financial Stability is the result of providing products and services that are both socially beneficial and economically profitable for the company and its stakeholders.

Certainly organizational crises occur; and when they do, a well-thought-out, documented and rehearsed crisis plan can be the difference between simply surviving or thriving. Recognizing vulnerabilities and developing strategies that address and mitigate them in advance is true reputation management. This approach can minimize damage and shorten the duration of a crisis.

Operationalizing Reputation Management

Unfortunately, organizations continue to struggle with how to manage reputational risks. Simply recognizing them isn't enough. So what do companies need to do? Centralize and create accountability for execution of the function, including:

- Articulate organizational values.
- Evaluate what's important to stakeholders.
- Assess how the organization performs.
- Inventory gaps (vulnerabilities).
- Build strategies to mitigate vulnerabilities.
- Monitor the change in beliefs and expectations.

Vulnerabilities exist within the supply chain, operations, the marketplace, internal culture, etc. As such, oversight has to be at the highest levels within an organization and be comprised of a cross-functional team who can create alignment with overall risk assessment, survey of directors.

Regardless of how an organization elects to manage reputational risk, it's clear it must be central, cross-functionally integrated and part of an overall risk management system.

Within a few hours, a huge corporation's reputation can be damaged to such an extent that it can take months, if not years, to recover.

"The way to gain a good reputation is to endeavor to be what you desire to appear." – **Socrates**

If you're a business, reputation management is an important part of your life. Thanks to the Internet and social media, it's easy for customers to disseminate good or bad information to an increasingly-large audience. Be prepared. Establish a response plan, and build a solid foundation for your reputation. And, above all, when crises arise, take action quickly.

Public distrust of corporations, along with increased regulation and demand for transparency, has heightened the need for organizations to invest in corporate reputation management and changed the role and expectation of senior leaders.

Increasingly, top business leaders understand the importance of corporate reputation. For the second year in a row, reputational risk ranked as the No. 1 concern (other than financial risk) by boards of directors.

Managing corporate reputation starts by helping the board of directors, CEO and senior leadership to understand – or help define – the vision, mission, values and strategy of the organization, which underscores the organization's strategic direction.

Three key areas in an organization must be aligned to build stakeholder trust and a positive reputation: operations, social impact, and financial stability.

Corporate reputation = business operations, positive social impact, and financial stability.

Analyze the gaps between how an organization sees itself, how it wants to be seen, and how it is perceived by its key stakeholders. Design a program that manages your corporate reputation to close the gaps. You must develop a strategic reputation management plan that includes: listening and discovery, strategy-planning, execution, and measurement.

With Reputation Management, it's essential for you to take charge of cultivating a positive reputation for your brand. It can make the difference between getting the kind of business opportunities your company deserves and missing out.

When you're getting started managing your reputation be sure to consider the following guidelines:

- Decide ahead of time what you want to share so that you can remain consistent and protect privacy.
- Understand that transparency is for brands, not people. Transparency is something only brands have to consider. Being transparent refers more to when a company has a defective product

and needs to report what's happened and what's being done about it to the public without holding back information.

• Decide that prevention is the best cure. Paying attention to what you're presenting to the world via a Google search is key to preventing reputation management trouble. Create opportunities to share valuable, good news about your brand.

• Be prepared. One of the best things you can do to strengthen your online reputation management strategy is to brainstorm for nightmare scenarios with a senior level team. Think about worst-case scenarios and what the best remedies and plans of action would be for that event.

How to Respond to an Online-Reputation Crisis

When it comes to managing an online-reputation crisis, remember this adage: An ounce of prevention is worth a pound of cure. But if you're in the middle of a crisis that could damage your brand, you need to take action.

No matter what your situation, consider the following:

• Spot the issue as early as possible via monitoring. Respond to people in real time as much as possible. Never leave people hanging for long, or else they will tend to share more emotionally. This is how issues escalate.

• Be transparent via your brand. If there's a problem … admit to it, apologize, and tell what's being done to address the problem.

• Keep people up to date. As new developments arise, let people know online.

• At every chance, look for opportunities to learn and improve from feedback.

Trying to appease a troublemaker makes them bolder. Set boundaries for what your brand will and won't do in order to make people happy, and stick by them.

The process of reputation management: With the explosion of social media websites, companies must also manage their online reputation. This means that your company needs to have clean, appropriate, and accurate social media accounts. They must provide

visitors with answers to questions and offer a clear view of your
company.

Update Company Skeleton Profile

All companies have what is called a skeleton profile on the
Internet. The skeleton profile is found in an online business directory
that has published your phone number, physical address, website,
e-mail address or other information.

There are plenty of skeleton profiles out there that are inaccurate.
They include the wrong information or outdated information of
companies. Check your skeleton profile and make sure it has accurate
contact information for your business.

Maintain Your Social Media Profiles

Maintain the company social media profiles as the company
evolves. Companies change logos, mottoes, etc. Be sure to edit all of
these when your company puts them into action. Update your social
media accounts to keep pace with your company's brand, dates.

All of your company's social media sites should link to each other.
This is a way to cross-promote your company.

Reputation Management: What Does Your Online Presence Say to Prospects?

Link to Positive Content

Every time there is a press release or news article highlighting your
company in a positive light, be sure to link to this content on your
website and social media pages.

In today's social world, managing your online reputation is more
critical than ever to protect your company's brand; and one thing is
certain: everyone needs a plan. Your company pushes forward your
brand's online goals, and is able to deal with negative chatter.

What Is Online Reputation Management?

Online reputation management is the process of ensuring that
the right information appears when people look up the name of your

brand in search engines like Google and Bing, or on social networks like Facebook, Twitter, or LinkedIn. The idea is to minimize negative content and to promote flattering content.

As new media evolves, the strongest brands will be those that listen closely to what people are saying and who respond quickly with messages that show they are listening and that they understand.

Major problems can come up that could jeopardize your brand. Here are two real-life examples:

• Embarrassing viral videos. When someone gets the bright idea to upload an embarrassing video, it can make even his employer look bad. If a video also divulges unflattering corporate secrets, it can inspire viral outrage. Example: Pink Meat, taking a bath in the restaurant's sink, licking a stack of tortillas, etc.

• Disaster strikes. During one airplane crisis, online outrage gushed as hard as the leak and for much longer.

Using Analytics

Analytics can tell you a lot about the kinds of people who are coming to visit you online and what they do when they get to your site. Analytics applications:

• Track what site your visitors came from.

• How long visitors stayed at your site.

• How many pages they visited, and which ones.

Brand reach: Anytime more people hear good things about your brand, you've extended your brand reach in a positive way.

Sales: A trustworthy reputation can often help sell more of your product online.

Product development: You have access to amazing market research in social networks and blogs.

Consider these goals:

• Increasing your brand awareness.

• Acquiring new customers.

• Boosting business outcomes.

• Responding to customer service questions and concerns in a more personal way.

• Positioning your brand where your target audiences are.

• Identifying your organization as the go-to brand online for your product line. Why wait for the competition to beat you there?

• Early adopters are always rewarded if a network becomes popular.

How to Build and Protect Your Digital Reputation

When your company uses the Internet, social media, or any other channels, make sure your company is careful to do so in accordance with your values, policies, and the requirements of law. You also need to take good care of your company's digital reputation – to exercise good judgment and to be thoughtful, so that your digital profile accurately reflects the one they want others to see.

Digital reputation is the online image you present about your company through all digital means: social computing platforms, blogs, websites, e-mail, mobile devices, etc.

Each company is responsible for their digital reputation, and should carefully and actively manage their reputation in the digital world, a world where information and images you post can go public and spread rapidly and can be seen by everyone.

Reputation is important, and reputation online is an extension of a company's professional image. It is critical that companies take the time to nurture and protect their digital reputation, and make informed decisions about what content they allow themselves to be linked to.

Companies can manage their digital reputation by crafting, protecting, and maintaining an online image that provides a positive view regarding their overall character. They can greatly enhance their reputation by constantly working to engage in discussions in digital spaces to build and strengthen relationships.

In seeking to manage and build your digital reputation, abide by these high-level principles:

Your reputation is your brand. Treat your reputation as a highly-valued asset in your company's portfolio. Be strategic and careful regarding what content to allow your company to be linked to; everything you post or allow to be posted should be in support of building your digital reputation.

Think before you post. If you have doubts about the appropriateness of content, don't post it or let it be posted. Information can spread quickly and widely and can stay on the Internet for a long time. Consider the implications of material to your digital reputation and whether or not you would want that material to still be visible in ten years.

Remain positive and constructive. Contribute content that is helpful and thoughtful in all situations. Don't make derogatory or inflammatory comments about other individuals or organizations. These statements can come back to tarnish your reputation. Being negative doesn't build credibility.

Strive for professionalism. As a rule of thumb, anything that would be inappropriate to say or do in public settings, such as the office, is inappropriate behavior on social networks.

Consider the long-term. Any reputation takes time to build, and a digital reputation is no exception. As previously mentioned, content posted online can remain there for a long time – make sure that the content posted about your company builds a history of professionalism and insightful content.

Demographic analytics have the ability to track geo-specific changes and unravel new markets.

Behavioral analytics are used to identify users, detractors, influencers, and recommenders to track brand and reputation management.

Reputations can be managed, but doing so requires diligence and integration into the overall operational and risk management structure. It requires governance and leadership to succeed.

We can send you more information to get your company on track for reputation management by scheduling a telephone call on our website.

Contact Joe (JT) Ippolito
http://www.mediamarketingmgmt.com

http://www.jtippolito.com
http://www.linkedin.com/in/mediamarketingmanagement/

Biography

Joe (JT) Ippolito is a former executive for IBM, Xerox, AT&T, and NEC. He is the Founder and CEO of Media Marketing Management. As an award-winning entrepreneur, business owner, speaker, author, and consultant, he specializes in cross-channel marketing strategies that help companies increase their revenue with his proprietary tactics.

His websites are located at: http://www.mediamarketingmgmt. com and http://www.jtippolito.com.

Joe has worked on complex technology solutions with C-level executives in boardroom settings. Having received numerous awards, clients have included: Disney, Mattel, Sony, Warner Bros., and Fox.

A self-styled "media disrupter," Joe's ideas challenge the status quo of new media marketing. For 34 years, he's dedicated his career to his unique brand of high-leverage marketing, bringing great success to former employers and dozens of name-brand clients.

Chapter 4: Productive Employees and Lifelong Customers with Webinars

Internal and External Growth Strategies of the Fortune 500

by Melodie Rush

Back in 2001 I found myself in quite a dilemma. I was one of two technical sales people in the world supporting a software product. The two of us were overworked and not able to meet the needs of our customers or the account executives. As an employee I wasn't happy and, of course, our current and potential customers were not happy because of the delay in meeting their needs.

Then one day I received an email from our corporate IT department informing me of a new resource that was being made available to us. This resource was an online service that would allow us to do presentations over the Internet. Could this be the solution to our shortage of staff? I was intrigued and set about to learn how to use this service.

In 2001 I had not heard of webinars and certainly had not attended one. And to be honest there were very few resources to help in my understanding and comprehension of how to use webinars. So through trial and error we begin to utilize webinars. Before I dive into more details about them, let's first cover what webinars are.

What Is a Webinar?

The term webinar is a contraction of "web" plus "seminar." So, simply stated, they are seminars presented online over the web. Early on this meant the presenter was able to screen share and show slides, applications or web pages to attendees. The audio was transmitted via phone lines.

Later on, other terms like "webcast" and "web conference" started to appear. The term webcast is a contraction of web plus broadcast, so think of these more like a newscast or talk show. For a webcast, video is streamed over the Internet, which means the attendees can see live video of you or of video you play.

A web conference is group collaboration over the web. This is much like a department meeting that is conducted over the web, where attendees can collaborate on documents as well as discuss important issues. These can be done with or without video streaming, and with or without screen, application or document sharing.

Initially these three – webinar, webcast and web conference – were differentiated by the technology running underneath the services. Over the last several years, the lines have blurred and pretty much all services offer the ability to do video streaming (you can be seen live over the web), screen share (share what is on your computer screen), and communication between presenters and/or attendees either through phone or computers over the Internet.

For the rest of this chapter I will use the term webinar as a general term to represent all three of these.

Productive Employees

How can webinars be utilized to help employees be more productive? For the last 15 years I have seen webinars used more and more in improving employee productivity and employee satisfaction. In today's global economy, webinars provide companies with the ability to reach their employees whether they are located locally or remotely for onboard training, staff meetings, and to create opportunities for employee productivity gains.

Onboard training starts with new-employee orientation and continues with ongoing employee education for new services, products and software being offered or adopted by the company. By utilizing webinars companies can roll out new company initiatives quickly at a lower cost. And because everyone can attend the training at the same time, conversion to new systems can be achieved in a quicker time frame.

Webinars also are used for weekly, monthly, quarterly or annual staff meetings. By utilizing webinars employees can be kept up to date on important company news and announcements. Department or project meetings can be conducted where employees can collaborate on documents and projects at a push of the button, thus making these meetings way more productive than having to pass documents around and potentially missing vital recommendations or corrections.

Most important are the productivity gains achieved by using webinars in day-to-day activities. Webinars help employees save time in several ways, first and foremost by less travel. Travel can mean travel from location to location by car, plane, train, or even more importantly by foot. Employees traveling between buildings or from their office to a conference room often take up to several minutes or longer depending on the distractions and detours they may take. By being able to join meetings from their office over the Internet it cuts down on these distractions and saves time that can be used for better purposes.

Because employees can attend remotely, it allows meetings to include all employees that might not otherwise have been able to participate in person. This brings better collaboration and synergy to projects and department and companywide meetings.

With the proliferation of smartphones and tablets, employees can also attend webinars on these devices. This gives them even greater access to the information being shared and increased ability to participate and collaborate.

One of the most powerful features of webinars is the ability to record. This allows employees to watch and listen to meetings or trainings they were unable to attend live at a time that works for them. It also allows for those who did attend to be able to review for clarification or to enhance notes and their understanding of the content covered.

Webinars are one of the most cost-efficient tools to help with employee productivity, retention, and overall satisfaction.

Lifelong Customers

How can webinars be used to ensure lifelong customers? Webinars can be used in many customer retention initiatives including marketing campaigns, training, technical support, sales, consulting and general knowledge transfer exchanges. The two that people are most familiar with are marketing and sales.

For marketing, webinars are used for brand awareness, new leadership, product and service announcements, lead generation, customer feedback, and focus groups. All of these things contribute to improving customer relationships. Webinars allow marketing to interact and engage customers globally. Customers who feel heard are way more likely to stick with a company's products and services.

The sales teams utilize webinars to increase revenue by reaching new customers and educating existing customers about new products or services. Webinars allow them to bring together people from different departments and even different parts of the world. These meetings ensure that everyone is onboard with any new service or product that the company is investing in. It also often shortens the sales cycle as potential customers quickly see the benefits and are able to ask questions and resolve objections more quickly.

Webinars are also used by Education to facilitate both free and paid training. Webinars allow instructors to interact with students by teaching material and testing their comprehension. Courses can range from an hour to several days. As universities have moved to online degree programs, more and more people have adopted and sought out online training from companies. This training not only becomes a revenue stream for the company but also helps customers become more loyal as they are able to understand and use their knowledge with the product or service.

Support or technical support, depending on the nature of the product or service, uses webinars to show customers how to solve problems as well as being able to have customers show their issue or challenge. This interaction is beneficial for both sides, as oftentimes the customer cannot accurately describe the issue they are having or have issues implementing the solution support sends them. I have seen webinars significantly reduce the resolution time of customer issues.

Companies that offer consulting services utilize webinars similarly to how support does but also use webinars to manage projects with customers. Webinars are often used for weekly, monthly or quarterly update meetings as well as a collaboration tool for the project team.

Another way that webinars are used effectively to improve customer loyalty is to provide ongoing information or knowledge transfer sessions. These sessions can include topics like what's new, tips and tricks, deeper dive into subjects, and ask the expert. The sessions can also be recorded and be offered as on-demand so that customers that are unable to attend live will be able to consume the session at a later date when they have time.

And just like for employees, the ability to watch webinars over smartphones or tablets makes the information you want to share with your customers even more accessible.

The rest of the story...

In 2001, I started using webinars to help my company meet the needs of our customers and account executives because of a staff shortage. My coworker and I decided instead of doing individual onsite presentations for each customer, we would offer a webinar once a week with the product overview information. We set up the webinars and sent the links to the account executives and they invited all of their prospects to the meeting each week.

This became a huge success. In fact, even though I left that position close to 10 years ago these webinars are still done every Friday and have at least 25 attendees each week. Imagine if you could attract 25 or more new leads to your product or service each week.

Not only did I use webinars in this capacity, I have also presented using webinars to many of the Fortune 500 companies both for pre-sales and retention activities. In fact we use webinars for training paid and free, internal and external meetings, technical support of the products, consulting projects, sales, and more.

In the past 15 years I have continued to utilize webinars to train and educate both coworkers and clients and have conducted well over 1500 webinars to groups from 1 to 500 attendees. I have sold products and services from a few thousand dollars to over a million dollars as well as saved cancellation of products utilizing webinar technology. In my opinion and experience, webinars are the single most important tool to help companies efficiently communicate and reach both their employees and customers.

Over the years the technology has improved vastly from the early days where we could only screen share showing slides on our desktop and transmit audio over a phone line. Now we are able to do live video and audio streaming over the Internet. We have tools within the webinar services that allow us to conduct chats, polls and even give presentations or collaboration or computer control rights to anyone that attends.

Almost everyone who works for a company of any size has attended webinars on a regular basis either with their company or through their personal hobbies or interests, so they are familiar with the technology.

I've been fortunate to not only utilize webinars as an employee but also to help others learn and utilize webinars in their businesses. I help presenters and facilitators run successful webinars by teaching them the before, during and after skills needed to be effective in reaching their audience, keeping their audience engaged, and following up with their audience afterward.

Companies that utilize webinars in their day-to-day business are able to have much more productive employees and build the relationship for lifelong customers.

Enjoy a complimentary copy of my international best-selling book *Deliver Webinars Like a Pro* at http://book.deliverwebinars.com and join my Facebook group at https://www.facebook.com/groups/deliverwebinars to learn more about webinars.

Connect with Melodie Rush

www.melodierush.com

www.facebook.com/wecreatemvps

https://twitter.com/WeCreateMVPs
https://www.linkedin.com/in/melodierush
https://plus.google.com/+MelodieRush1
https://www.facebook.com/groups/deliverwebinars
Podcast – *The Webinar Report* https://itunes.apple.com/us/podcast/
the-webinar-report/id981327747
http://www.stitcher.com/s?fid=65581&refid=stpr
www.deliverwebinarsbook.com
www.webinarmasteryb2p.com/product1

Bonus Material

Enjoy a complimentary copy of my international best-selling book
Deliver Webinars Like a Pro at http://book.deliverwebinars.com and
join my Facebook group:

https://www.facebook.com/groups/deliverwebinars/ to learn
more about webinars.

Biography

Melodie Rush is a trained Statistician and holds a technical MBA. She has presented and consulted with many Fortune 500 companies both domestically and internationally. Being a geek has not always been cool, but it has certainly given her the opportunity to teach and consult on many analytical topics across many industries. Her biggest strength is relating technical information to nontechnical folks.

Melodie has an uncanny ability to simplify topics and chunk them into small bite-size pieces that even those afraid of analytics can understand. Melodie is an experienced speaker both live and virtual via webinars, having led more than 1500 webinars since 2001. She knows what works and what doesn't when it comes to doing presentations.

She is the best-selling author of the book *Deliver Webinars Like a Pro*. Melodie launched "We Create MVPs" to share her knowledge and expertise by helping those new to webinars become powerful, influential presenters. Additionally, Melodie works with her clients to become recognized experts in their chosen niche through video, social media and online marketing.

Her experience includes creating and implementing surveys, analyzing data, coordinating presentations from 1 hour to three days. Melodie lives in Colorado with her husband and two cats. She loves to travel, scrapbook, and play with technology. In her spare time, she volunteers at the Denver Zoo as a Docent.

Chapter 5: The Social CEO

Online Strategies Designed, Tested, and Destined for Success

by Olivier Taupin and Sharon A.M. MacLean

Chapter Synopsis

In the time it has taken you to read this sentence, 50,000 tweets have been sent. How many of those messages might mention your company name with an industry hashtag – good or bad? This chapter is for those CEOs who study rather than avoid change in the marketplace. It's for those leaders who want to "get the story right" by adopting best social media practices tailored for their organization … reviewing competitors' strategies … and using social media as a rallying point for employees. Getting people to know and trust you doesn't happen overnight in personal dealings. The same is true for growing your business in online networks.

Here's your QuickMap to 10 Steps for Social Leadership – The Taupin Model ©

The above is linked to the PDF supplied. (http://media. instantcustomer.com/22902/0/199_10-steps-social-media-leadership. pdf)

＊ ＊ ＊ ＊ ＊

Remarkable, isn't it? We're talking about the many challenges you've met through your leadership role in the C-suite. You've had to evaluate opportunities, manage risk, find talent, scale efficiently, stay on top of government regulations – and nurture trust within your key circles of influence.

We're also talking about the colossal cultural and economic changes that arrived in lockstep with social media. And why becoming a Social CEO is essential for the growth of your company.

Let's start with the research. Studies from MBA Central (http://www.mbacentral.org/ceos-social-media/) increasingly report that executives (76%) today would rather work for a Social CEO than for a leader who insists on remaining a Luddite. MBA Central also revealed that three out of four customers say a company is more trustworthy if its high-level management participates in the digital sphere.

Weber Shandwick, a leading global public relations firm, released 2015 survey results that asked 50 of the world's largest companies about their attitudes regarding social media. The firm found that CEO sociability has more than doubled since 2010 when only 36% of CEOs were social. Weber Shandwick defined CEOs as "social" if they did one of the following:

- Opened a public and verifiable social network account on Facebook, Twitter, and LinkedIn.
- Engaged on the company website through messages, pictures, or video.
- Appeared in a video on the company YouTube channel.
- Authored an external blog.

What About Risk Management?

This is where it gets sticky. Only 10% of leadership indicated confidence in their general counsel's ability to handle social media risk. FCI Consulting reported the results in their recent study titled *Our Law in the Boardroom*. The low trust reflects an apprehension about how easy it is for employees and competitors to comment in public – without controls in place – about your company.

Yet, the metric also points to the importance of returning to fundamentals with respect to your employees, noted Erica Salmon Byrne, head of Advisory Services and Research at NYSE Governance in Services. "Do they understand what's expected of them in this newer medium?" she asked. "Do they know the risks? And will they tell you when something has gone wrong?"

The take-away for the C-suite, reports MBA Central, is that your competitors use social tools to learn everything possible about your enterprise (13%); seek insights from third-party influencers (40%); and track crisis situations (44%) through evidence-based research. It's for these reasons that we encourage you to place social media on the priorities agenda – fast.

Age of Authenticity

It's difficult to miss: The contemporary phrase "authentic behavior" is repeated everywhere today. Your customers, the media and the wider community are pretty good at spotting phony responses and they want a leader who is real.

The hurdle for mature business people is knowing that certain messages are not always accurate. Many spent an entire life positioning their company in the best possible light, sometimes by omitting details that could harm a carefully-constructed image. This habit of covering up troublesome facts leads to big challenges in a world where empowered customers want candid, plain-spoken and genuine governance. In a Google World, consumers want mistakes to be recognized and they expect to see apologies accompanied by sincere forms of rectitude.

Here's how 3 executives define authenticity.

Kyle Sherwin, VP of Media, Sony Music: *"The original 'idea' of authenticity was essentially a way for corporations to attempt to not sound corporate in their marketing efforts – or at the very least to stay true to their essence."*

Rick Maynard, Senior Manager of Public Relations, KFC: *"To us, being real means being honest, inclusive, boldly unapologetic, refreshingly to the point, insightful and, occasionally, a little edgy. We steer clear of being artificial, judgmental, insecure, full of hot air, timid or gimmicky."*

Joe Barbagallo, Social Media Manager, Volvo Cars US: *"Authentic means being transparent. We know our audience knows us well, and so we have to be honest. You've got to be forthright, especially if consumers are asking you a question."*

People want to know what drives your passion. Because if you can drill down to the very essence of why you deliver your products and services, that clarity makes us care, too. It's captivating – and makes us want to follow your parade.

Authenticity is real. It's serious enough for the Pulitzer-winning Guardian newspaper to run a headline that said, "The fastest way to kill your brand: Inauthenticity."

As co-writers of this chapter, we reflected on how social media evolved to influence organizations. Olivier and I first met in 2009 through LinkedIn, the network for professionals that launched in 2004. I owned and published a regional magazine that covered leaders of commerce and the community in Alberta, Canada. Olivier – who lived near Seattle – was interviewed by a senior writer assigned to explain how social media could impact the oil and gas sector in my country. Olivier, already a social media authority, owned the largest group on LinkedIn and had originated professional rules of engagement for groups. The magazine flew off the stands.

My intent for assigning the story was to wake up the oil and gas sector, especially in Alberta, as to how new communications methods could share a positive story with the world. Industry consultant and writer Ken Chapman took on the assignment in a most prescient way. In the cover story, he said, "The Internet culture hates broadcasting and spam, but it loves authentic virtual relationships ... and those generate word-of-mouth messaging from friends and influentials."

Olivier was the best person to interview because he owned Linked:HR, the largest professional group in the network. That group today has one million members. Other groups he founded include Linked:Energy with 220K members while 121K people joined Next Dimension Careers. Today, the visionary shows leaders how to socialize their organizations from top-to-bottom and is at the front line of tomorrow's social media: vertical networks. I sold *Edmontonians* in 2010 – soon after publishing the feature on LinkedIn – to lead an online start-up in wellness. Today, I coach and consult with organizational leaders who don't want to get left behind.

Olivier and I recognize how ignoring social media allows others to shape the narrative. Taking back control means writing your own story before others define it for you. Here's how to start.

Stage 1: Mindset

Confusion reigns when social media is not aligned with
the corporate vision, mission, and strategic objectives. If all the
departments are constantly tripping over each other, the promise of
your brand becomes an empty pledge. Worse, a brand can derail if not
coordinated in social media. This means that representation comes
from sales, marketing, operations, customer support, IT, and HR.

Each department may be using social media, but employees
are using different networks for reasons known only to them. For
example, branding gets confused when HR considers the company
culture to be traditional in nature but IT staff regard themselves as
forward-thinking while PR delivers still another profile to investors
and the media.

As you assume the mantle of Social CEO, watch out for these
situations that could thwart your efforts.

This is an increasingly-common request: **"We want you to
manage our social media."** There are great expectations for product
launches and frantic calls to promote attendance at special events –
yet, relationships haven't been established to help share the messages
in networks such as LinkedIn, Twitter, Facebook or Instagram and
Pinterest. The CRM's email database is incomplete, too.

**"We have an event in two weeks and need a Twitter
campaign to fill the room."** Alarmingly, this is a familiar call. The
challenge is the company has insufficient followers which leads to
reliance on the network belonging to an outside social media specialist
or the temptation of buying lists. It never works because the vendor's
followers generally have nothing to do with your business. Don't get
us wrong: It is possible to generate much interest with little advance
notice using certain tactics, but those relationships are shaky and likely
won't last.

**"Our sales reps know our customers well. They take them
golfing all the time."** You may know your clients well after years of
long-time service; but there will be trouble going forward finding new
clients prospects. Customers retire … move on … change positions.
It's always a good idea to take relationships offline … yet, it's also

imperative to develop the online sales funnel where new prospects are living today.

"My company doesn't have a social media plan, but I'm pretty good." Yes, individuals may have connections here and there on various networks, but the overall company is entirely disconnected. The future belongs to the corporation that recognizes its strength is the sum of personal brands belonging to all who work there.

It's time to set up a collaborative group drawn from key departments because social media is everybody's business. Here's your start-up checklist.

1. **Lead by example.** This is not the time for passing the buck with this statement: "I don't use social media but our folks have it covered." Embrace social media yourself, learn how the platforms work, and how they can drive a company's success or failure.

2. **Interview board members and management to determine their level of understanding of social business.** Too much social media is being created from the bottom-up in organizations which means core messages get lost amidst the blur of comments posted on multiple channels.

3. **Conduct an audit.** Learn which networks your employees have joined on behalf of the company, determine their activity level, and whether messages are aligned. The initial part of the report analyzes the company's brand in addition to official and unofficial social media accounts belonging to the CEO.

Learn how each of these accounts perform. Unofficial accounts are sent to the legal team for investigation. Potential customers, employee candidates and stakeholders may be influenced in damaging ways by bogus profiles.

The second part of the report identifies the main social media accounts of industry leaders, competitors, and social influencers. This will be used to weigh the social media influence of the company and CEO against the best influencers in the company's markets.

1. **Build a cross-functional social media department that reports to the CEO (SMB) or Chief Social Media Officer (Enterprise).** This department is structured around the newly-

appointed Social Media Architect in charge of orchestrating all social media campaigns. The Social Media Architect and the Content Architect are in charge of directing the creation, acquisition and delivery of multimedia content and delivery. Both Architects have dotted-line relationships with all department and business unit managers with social media responsibilities.

2.   **Link everybody.** CEOs are linked to their direct report and one level lower. All employees are linked to their team lead which makes up the umbrella group for social media. This helps the entire company know what each other is saying and doing in the networks, implement a rapid response strategy when required, and immediately handle customer service requests.

3.   **Train your employees and then trust them.** Host regular company webinars/seminars to update employees, deliver general information materials including the annual report and on-boarding guidelines, send event hashtags and photos for sharing to employees together with corporate identity logos.

4.   **Establish Agile Monitoring and Control.** This updated approach to project management provides real-time reporting on several key metrics. Relevant and newsworthy information is sent to tablets and smartphones of other C-suite executives and key personnel.

Stage 2: Know Your people

The list of networks – each with its own personality, rules of engagement, and secrets to discover – now count over 800. More are added weekly. The Big 5 are LinkedIn, Twitter, Facebook, YouTube, and Google+; Instagram and Pinterest are strong in certain categories; and Periscope is picking up steam. Keep an eye on blab.im, as well. LinkedIn and Twitter are the two networks we favor for C-Suite business. Don't discount Facebook as a tool for business which still is favored in the B-to-C market.

1.   **Find the influencers among your employees.** These individuals could be authorities in a variety of subjects on Facebook and have major accounts on LinkedIn and Twitter. You will never know unless you carry out a social audit to discover how your

employees participate in their networks. Also think about reaching out to customers, partners and sponsors who have the potential to become company champions.

2.   **Implement an Employee Advocacy program.** An Employee Advocacy program is the best way to analyze employee social profiles without invading their privacy. Imagine the reach sparked by your company if 100 employees tweeted favorably on the arrival of a new vice president, launch of a new product, or results of a community event hosted by your company. Think about the powerful reach when everyone retweets!

3.   **Call for an Employee Influence Assessment Survey from the Social Media Architect.** Discover which employees are willing to participate in the company's social media programs.

- What are the social media accounts these social employees intend to use?
- Which of these social employees are "social media influencers?"

Kristina Cisnero, Online Strategist for Hootsuite Media, defines social media influencers as individuals who have "the power to influence others in their social media circle." She states that these influencers align with the company's business and that employees with "a website or blog that ranks high in the SERPs (search engine results page) usually have the best influencers you can find."

Finally, the Social Media Architect needs to identify unsocial employees and executives who need to be social in their position (where the CEO is #1 on the list). These are individuals who need additional social media training.

Employee Advocacy applications such as GaggleAMP make it easy to assess employee social influence while offering the privacy expected by those employees.

1.   **Educate your organization on influencer marketing and the use of social media.** Ask your learning and development management to develop a plan to train all employees and executives starting with the CEO. Here's why:

- Content published by influencers is considered worth their follower's time;
- Influencers engage their followers on topics of mutual interest;
- Experts keep themselves informed about their industry and form respected opinions on their industry.

2. **Enhance business development.** People expect brands to talk with them rather than at them. They no longer expect brands to sell to them, but to entertain and inform them. In every case, the CEO connects with key employees. The lines have blurred between offline and virtual life. This means there are many new opportunities to enhance your company by involving employees and champions as you grow together.

Bonus Material

Your QuickMap to Social Leadership. You're not the type of leader to back down from a challenge. If you need a custom-made plan to transform yourself and your organization into a forward-looking enterprise, we are delighted to help show you the way. Social Media Leadership -The Taupin Model © can be obtained at

http://media.instantcustomer.com/22902/0/199_10-steps-social-media-leadership.pdf

Biographies
Sharon MacLean

Sharon MacLean, President, WorldGate Media, believes we need entrepreneurs and industry leaders to thrive, and flourish, in our linked-up world.

As owner and publisher of a noted business magazine for 21 years, Sharon created content with forward-thinking solutions. An early adopter of social media, she positioned the magazine online using Twitter, Facebook, LinkedIn, and automated email marketing.

Sharon originated the famous "Sizzling Under 30" that celebrated 200 young business leaders, "Women in Business," "Family Business," "International Business," and "Visionaries in Technology," among others. The Canadian entrepreneur later led an investor-backed start-up in its mission to create a marketing portal for wellness experts.

The veteran strategist now helps successful business people adapt their traditional methods to social enterprise.

Olivier G. Taupin

Olivier G. Taupin is at the front line of tomorrow's social media: vertical business networks. He also is the architect of the *10-Step Social*

Media Leadership – The Taupin Model © which guides CEOs on how to assess, plan, develop, and lead the social influence and the media content of their social media strategy.

For Olivier, expanding a company's social influence is no different than boosting the membership of a community, and he knows about communities: He founded the one-million-member Linked:HR, the largest professional group on LinkedIn worldwide. He also is the inspiration and the process strategist behind more than one hundred large business communities including Linked:Energy with 230K members, Next Dimension Careers with 120K members, and Linked:Seattle with 54K members.

Olivier lives at the foot of Mount Rainier, near Seattle, Washington. He is blessed to have been married for 20 years to his best friend and is the proud father of two highly-creative teenagers.

Chapter 6: Consistent Customer Retention?

Retaining Loyalty with Integrity-Leveraging Video Systems, Webcasts and Webinars

by Barry D. Gumaer, Sr., MBA

We almost found out the hard way how a simple ongoing video communication strategy could have prevented a near-disastrous end of a multi-decade customer association. It could also be beneficial in retaining our relationships with all our customers since "video moves business" by engaging and converting prospects and customers alike. At the end of the day, your business is about driving sales and keeping customers engaged and happy. Online video helps you do both. Here is a case in point.

Several years ago, we got a call from our biggest client stating he was extremely unhappy with the feedback and service he had been receiving of late and wanted us to know he was looking elsewhere for the products and services we had been providing his firm for more than 20 years. When I asked him why he was making the change after being such a long-term loyal customer, he simply said his company was feeling neglected, overlooked and underappreciated for the amount of business exchanged in our 20+-year relationship.

He also felt completely left out of the information and service processes. He told us we had been taking his company for granted and felt no one at our firm was interested enough to change the status quo and improve the relationship between the two companies.

We, in fact, had been neglecting this customer and others too, and had forgotten how important ongoing communication is and how the use of effective personal video messaging can be with all of our clients and customers to improve the success of both our company and theirs.

We immediately made an appointment to see him face-to-face and booked a flight in hopes of reconciling with our customer. Had we been proactive in our communications strategies and integrated personal video messages within our communications, our customer could have "seen and heard us" throughout the relationship, which could have effortlessly been maintained. We wouldn't have been in "panic mode" and been scrambling to repair this long-standing relationship.

We could have completely prevented this scenario had we followed simple steps and integrated targeted, very specific video messages in our communications with our customers. The overpowering message is: "Video moves and connects in business!"

Let's face it. Without loyal, happy customers, businesses cannot be sustained, be profitable, or grow. Consequently, retention becomes difficult for an enterprise if they don't maintain their integrity with customers. It's vital since retention benefits enterprise growth and profit. Connection and retention are an imperative, an integral component of the brand promise the company makes to the buyer. So when customers feel neglected or badly treated because of poor, infrequent or absence of interaction or access to product or service resolutions, the integrity of the firm is frequently questioned.

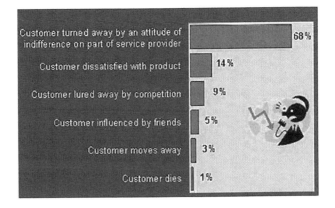

Customer turned away by an attitude of indifference on part of service provider	68%
Customer dissatisfied with product	14%
Customer lured away by competition	9%
Customer influenced by friends	5%
Customer moves away	3%
Customer dies	1%

It's important to remember:

- Customers want to feel important.
- Customers crave to be appreciated.
- Customers will not connect unless they feel valued by you.
- Customers have, on average, a very short attention span.
- Customers are drawn to those who show genuine interest.

68% of all customers leave because of poor attitude or indifference on the part of the service provider.

Customer Retention Methodologies

Customer retention is one key issue keeping corporate executives and management awake at night. Thus, maintaining and improving relationships with customers requires attitude shifts as well as strategy changes with a top-down approach starting in the C-Suite, considering this is a highly-sensitive and exceedingly-important issue.

Highly-effective strategic solutions involve communicative and expressive video assets, systems, and media. They are extremely effective in improving customer relationships, problem resolution and valued client retention. The most effective audiovisual strategies include:

- Webcasts / Videocasts / Livecasts / Intranet Broadcasts (live and archived)
- Webinars (sales vehicles) Podcasts
- Podcasts (video and/or audio)
- Video Newsletters (information, entertainment, sales)
- Video Blogs (contextual information)
- Video Testimonials (how lives are being changed)
- Video Bookcasts
- Video-filled Events – well-produced video content executed within conferences and meetings including noteworthy live productions with large widescreen-projection presentations
- Live Event Webstreams – broadcasts recorded, archived, repurposed
- Videos published and positioned in social media platforms
- Regularly-scheduled video information broadcasts
- Video-embedded Multimedia Messaging Services

Beginnings and Fundamentals

My interest in video and video production began in school in the mid-1960s. It started with an analog, black-and-white 1/2-inch reel-to-reel videotape recorder and a single vidicon-tube camera, which was used to record school sporting events and has evolved into the extensive production, presentation and use of digital video.

Having grown up watching movies every Saturday afternoon in the movie theaters my dad managed, I was captivated by the stories that were presented in the films on the big screen. As a kid, I didn't have the resources to make motion pictures, but was enamored with the creative storytelling process and frustrated at the same time with the complicated, expensive process needed to create stories like the ones I saw up on the screen.

The advent of consumer videotape recording devices changed all of that. Now it was cost-effective to produce and record stories, and this developed into a passion for learning how to use these technologies and a more than 40-year career of video creation, production, presentation and support in universities and in corporate environments and events. A formal university education mid-career added an MBA with a marketing concentration to the toolkit, and allowed me to position audio and video production skills with more-defined and targeted marketing expertise directly into the business arena.

This confluence of video and marketing allowed more qualified, targeted and engaging messages-to-markets, better-defined market segments, lead-capturing devices and systems, sales funnel drivers, creative and stronger positioning in branding for clients. Video and audio production, marketing, webcasting, livecasting, and project management are our strongest and most effective results-driven solutions!

For a complimentary Video Messaging Infographic and Video Marketing Systems checklist: http://Completeav.net/VideoConnections.html.

Focus on video solution-driven procedures and processes: automated videos with messages within systems, efficiently engaging and retaining customers in more cost-effective approaches. Properly executed, these messages, using the strength and engagement of live or recorded video media and the correct message-to-market positioning, benefit the organization with extensive returns:

Improved Communication – Continues ongoing "conversations" and connections with customers and clients 24/7; increased message frequency and "touches."

Customer Engagement – Active and ongoing; fills sales funnels with qualified leads and repeat customers; educates, informs and entertains; keeps customers engaged and "not feeling neglected."

Cost-Effective – Smarter, more advantageous approach to communicate with large and growing audiences; best "bang for your buck" use of time and resources.

Authority – Positions the company as the go-to business or service provider while reducing sales-sequence expense.

Credibility – Creates ongoing trustworthiness.

Sales Growth – Efficient way to continue sales or upsells; videos "do the selling" by starting or continuing the sales sequence within the system.

Monetization – Additional revenue streams; enhanced information, certifications, or ongoing product or service education.

Strategic – Faster way to expand brand reach; wider influence potential.

Metrics – Trackable and measurable results with each video-enhanced vehicle.

Core-Competencies – Showcases what you're good at and/or introduces new products and services; niche focus advantages.

Message to Market – Primary channels to send specific messages to highly-defined target markets or market segments.

Multi-Purposed Content – Video can be broadcast in real-time or recorded and repurposed and used in multiple media, channels and forms such as audio downloads, transcripts, newsletters, podcasts and/or books depending upon how customers learn or want to consume information.

Social Media – Including videos in social media postings increases frequency, reach and engagement and can be seen anywhere around the world.

Production Value – Video can be produced in-house or outsourced and "done for you" or "done with you" depending on individual requirements, deadlines and resources.

Specialization – Video messages, content and vehicles are essential and, most significantly, THEY WORK!

Impact of Video

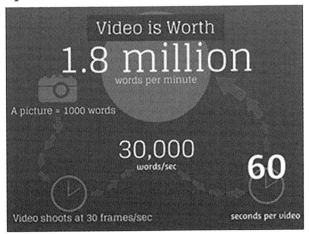

A picture equals **1,000** words. Video shoots **30 frames per second**. Therefore, every second of video is worth **30,000** words. Multiply **30k by 60 seconds** – a common length for an explainer video – and you get **1.8 million words per minute**. – *How Video Will Take Over the World* ©**2008 Forrester Research, Inc.**

A great example of the effectiveness and impact of video is Google-owned YouTube.com:

- 60 hours of video are uploaded every minute, or one hour of video is uploaded to YouTube every second.
- More than 4 billion videos are viewed a day.

- More than 800 million unique users visit YouTube each month.
- More than 3 billion hours of video are watched each month on YouTube.
- More video is uploaded to YouTube in one month than the 3 major U.S. television networks created in 60 years.
- 70% of YouTube traffic comes from outside the U.S.
- YouTube is localized in 39 countries and across 54 languages.
- In 2011, YouTube had more than 1 trillion views.
- In 2011 there were almost 140 views for every person on Earth.

This illustration sets up the predominance of video utilization, which effectively leads to....

Customer Engagement

Customer retention is driven by customer engagement. Video messages and video mediums do the engaging with your customers 24/7, when no one from the company is available. They create and sustain systematized relationships through video-enhanced messages! Webcasts or livecasts are as effective and efficient when live communication is required and customer locations are geographically unfavorable. Recordings of these events can be used for review, training, follow-up and knowledge reinforcement as well. They can be translated into many different languages to continue successful engagement with international audiences.

When customers are dissatisfied, disengaged or feel companies are simply neglecting them, a video message, newsletter or webcast communiqué can bridge the communication gap with news, information and/or added support. If these are long-term customers, they are most likely "relationship buyers" who need to be engaged continually and frequently by suppliers and not on a transaction-by-transaction basis.

Video webcasts, newsletters or blogs can similarly fill the gap cost-effectively and engage or re-engage customers.

Feedback and questions can be answered during live webinars or livecasts; and additionally, prompt responses through targeted questions can be posted on the company's blog.

Video in the digital age gives customers resources and beneficial information they can use to their advantage to make decisions in a quick, timely and cost-efficient manner. Video messages positioned to meet individual customer needs enable them to make faster decisions and choose different suppliers if their needs are not being met, or learn who will better serve and communicate with them.

Video webcasts provide a more responsive method to engage customers by crafting messages for rapid responses to a wider number of customers or larger audience, increasing engagement and feedback through the use of these improved methods, video media and technologies. New video toolsets are constantly being created and systems are being expanded and improved. The overriding message here is: engage, engage, and engage!

It follows then that video use and live webcasting in particular are essential elements in managing customer expectations in the retention process while maintaining organizational transparency and integrity. Customer retention strategies using video campaigns need to include the following essentials and messages to be delivered effectively.

1. **Exceed expectations.** Personalize your videos for your services. Instead of promising more than you can give, give more than you promise – under-promise, over-deliver. Deliver a "wow" customer experience. Video can do this consistently!

2. **Video can always be available.** Be there to serve customers with messages and information whenever they need you to be there. The Internet has enabled companies to have a constant presence with their customers, "24/7." Reliability and availability are vital. Make sure your customers know your video information is available on demand. Be involved in the same social media channels with videos as are your customers.

3. **Customize how you serve.** Find or develop video solutions that fulfill your individual customers' specific needs. Successful companies customize their business relationships with customers. They pride themselves on their one-on-one interactions. Their

salespeople value the differences in customer needs and respond with videos for customized solutions.

4. **Be easy to deal with.** Make doing business with you easy and pleasurable. A video presence can assume the burden of relieving inevitable aggravations for your customers. Companies who use video exceed their customers' expectations and do so by creating hassle-free experiences.

5. **Put the customer first.** Don't wait for opportunities to present themselves. Seek them out. Give customers more than they expect. Use video messages as a go-to resource to educate, entertain, inform and connect.

6. **Resolve conflicts and solve problems.** When conflicts arise, some companies have a tendency to deny them, debate them, shift responsibility for them, place blame for them, or hold their breath hoping they'll go away. Top salespeople accept ownership of the problem, collaborate on a solution, and take on the burden of finding a resolution regardless of fault. Video collaboration bridges the communication gap quickly and efficiently and benefits customer problem resolution and retention.

7. **Handle complaints.** Complaints usually have some validity and can be an "early warning system" of conflict on the horizon. When you view complaints this way, they can become your ally, helping you resolve problems and minimize their impact. Complaints that go unattended may evolve into conflicts that could have been avoided. Video conferences or interactive webcasts are a valuable tool to quickly get in front of customers and effectively handle complaints before they become more serious problems.

8. **Communicate constantly.** Ask questions that result in a dialogue. The more the customer talks, the more you'll learn. Continue questioning until you understand and have uncovered all the information required to proceed. Interactive videocasts, webcasts and video newsletters continue to "engage, engage engage." Avoid jumping to conclusions with customers. Ask them in person or via a videoconference!

9. **Remember nonverbal communication.** When communicating with customers using live video methods, observe

their non-verbal signals. Take note of their body language, appearance and posture. Look for signs of distraction. Pay attention to their facial expressions and eye contact. Listen to the tone of their voice as a means for understanding what they may be feeling. When you can't be there "in person," be there "live" via video!

Adapted from the book How You Do ... *What You Do: Create Service Excellence that Wins Clients for Life.* – **Bob Livingston**

These improved video media technologies are indispensible in the strategy of maintaining control over an important essential that is controllable within the corporation: Customer Retention.

These media are used as ongoing approaches to continue connecting and relating to customers who need to know FREQUENTLY they are important and meaningful to the enterprise. Each video technique, with a focused message to each market served, can have a direct impact on retaining customers, keeping them engaged and continuing to buy products and services.

They need to know they are important, have value and aren't just another number in a database. Their concerns, desires and requests need to be met and addressed while being communicated with appropriate timeliness and service. This is where advanced video strategies can be of great benefit in the engagement and retention of customers.

Video Techniques: What They Are with Benefits

Webcasts / Videocasts / Livecasts / Intranet Broadcasts (Live and Archived)

These are live, entertaining presentations broadcast over the Internet (or internal corporate intranet) using software-based systems to connect directly (or recorded replays), content-specific messages conveyed with person (CEO or others) on-camera and/or slides and additional videos as segments of the presentations that can be viewed via a web browser window on a desktop or laptop computer, tablet, phone or other mobile device.

Next to being face-to-face with either clients or employees (depending on the specific audience of the webcast), this is one of the best techniques to speak one-to-many with planned FREQUENCY without traveling away from the office or gathering the audience in one place.

One example would be regularly scheduled monthly or quarterly video content-specific communiqués (how-to's, tips, hints, thank-you's, interviews, testimonials, updates, instructional lessons, upcoming product releases, etc.) using video (think of the older video conference-type system) as an offensive strategy to continue engaging customers or employees.

Webcasts can leverage free services or use paid services. A video studio can be set up at a nominal cost using self-contained broadcasting systems or a laptop and streaming software and basic lighting, backdrops, monitors and audio enhancements (wireless microphones, mixing board, etc.).

Taking the time to implement this one strategy can have a noticeable improvement with customers since you have taken the time to show you care enough to connect with them in a much more personal way.

An additional module could also be added during webcasts if immediate feedback were needed. That would be the inclusion of a Chat function to enable customers to ask questions and interact during the live broadcast. The addition of this added tactic could provide abundant insight into what is on the minds of your customers.

Podcasts (Audio and/or Video)

Episodes and interviews uploaded to private channels on the Apple iTunes platform. These programs or episodes can be streamed via mobile devices or on laptops and desktops from specific "channels" on demand, or downloaded for consumption at a later time. Multiple subjects or channels can be created to facilitate differentiated audiences and customer market segments.

Webinars

Differentiated here from a webcast and defined as video approaches that can do all the things a webcast can do but is specifically used for instruction delivery and/or a sales vehicle. Many online services are available to broadcast your webcasts or webinars. These webinars should be very content-specific and targeted predominantly at specific customer niches or audiences.

Video Newsletters (Information, Entertainment, Education, and Sales)

Content-specific online newsletter embedded with video components, enhancing the overall newsletter experience and targeted at segmented customer audiences.

Video Blogs (Contextual Information)

Corporate blogs with embedded videos that enhance overall presentation. Content-specific vehicles targeted to specific market segments or customer audiences.

Video Testimonials (How Lives/Businesses Are Being Changed)

These videos are recorded from happy customers and/or employees and used in appropriate channels of distribution. Can be content-specific or general testimonial. Content-specific vehicles are targeted at specific audience segments.

Video Bookcasts (Authority-Positioning Vehicle with Interactive Inclusions)

This strategy consists of recorded content segments from a book, uploaded as chapters to video-sharing sites and used to drive traffic to websites and sales funnels. These videos can also be edited from live events and linked to lead pages for more information or a free report. These are content-specific vehicles targeted to specific or differentiated customer audiences.

Video-Filled Events – Major Productions (Widescreen); Webstreams (Live and Archived)

Content-specific off-site events and meetings for greatest initial impact and "wow" factor. They are targeted at specific customer segments and can be complimentary, by invitation only, or revenue-generating paid events.

Video Publishing Using Social Media

Content-specific and targeted at very specific audiences on many different social media sites including Facebook, Twitter, LinkedIn, Instagram, Pinterest, etc.

Regularly-Scheduled Video Broadcasts

Content-specific and targeted at very specific audiences and scheduled on specific days and times with scheduled frequency.

Multimedia Messaging Services

The videos created for MMS messages are no more than 15 seconds to play on a mobile phone or other mobile device and are scripted especially to elicit an action or response when the message is received. These are very content-specific and targeted at specific customers or market segments.

Each of the value-added video approaches presented here has a specific strategy for its implementation. The overall goal is to use video messaging, video webcasts, livecasts and effective video strategies to maintain relationships, improve and increase customer retention and trust, while preserving the integrity of the enterprise.

Producing loyal, satisfied customers is the ultimate goal to grow sales and increase profitability. The efficient technologies and systems available today allow increasingly cost-effective, customized, automated video messages and engagement. Video customization is key to customer retention.

If you develop your video messages, follow-up, and communication frequency correctly, integrity of the enterprise will not be in question. Engagement, retention and trustworthiness will be improved and maintained and be consistently profitable.

For a complimentary Video Messaging Infographic and Video Marketing Systems checklist: http://Completeav.net/VideoConnections.html.

Contact Barry D. Gumaer, Sr.

completeav@earthlink.net
https://linkedin.com/in/barrygumaersr
https://twitter.com/bgumaer

Bonus Material

For a complimentary Video Messaging Infographic and Video Marketing Systems checklist: http://Completeav.net/VideoConnections.html

Biography

Barry D. Gumaer, Sr., MBA, Digital Marketing Consultant, Producer, Speaker, Author. Barry is a highly-accomplished specialized marketer, author, speaker, consultant and digital video marketing consultant with highly-skilled proficiencies in marketing, lead generation, customer retentions, and an exceptional technical expertise in audio, video and creative production designs background in corporate meetings, events and entertainment, who brings results to the companies he consults.

He has been producing and directing videos since 1967 and uses his expertise to benefit varied enterprises in accomplishing their marketing and performance goals.

A serial entrepreneur since 1977, Barry has established businesses in video production, equipment and services; marketing; entertainment and retail; and web-specific design services.

Throughout a career of more than 40 years, he has worked with more than 350 of the Fortune 500 companies and executives including IBM, Disney, Boeing, Hershey, Sun Microsystems and CBS; past U.S. Presidents and other government officials including U.S. Supreme Court Justices; A-List celebrities; countless associations, medical societies, facilities and non-profit enterprises.

He works with local establishments in every conceivable category of business enterprise, specializing in enterprises with revenue of $1 to $15 million, furthering their efforts toward increasing customers, revenues and ROI.

Barry D. Gumaer, Sr., MBA, is the President/CEO of Complete AV, LLC, a marketing solutions consulting company specializing in Video Marketing Solutions, website and Direct Response marketing services and video production. Established in 1983, it is based in Palm Springs, California.

Guiding Statement

"When the student is ready ... the teacher appears!"

Chapter 7: Customer Loyalty

Keeping It Personal in the Digital World

by Pat Ziemer

Customer service, like everything else, has changed dramatically in recent years. When I started my business career 40 years ago as a co-owner of three funeral homes, our primary customer service tools were the telephone, personal contact with families, and a "request for comments" card sent to families after services.

While the comment card tactic was very basic, by reviewing and compiling the comments we were able to determine that 20% of the families did not know who they would use as a funeral provider in advance of needing the services. We were able to use this information to tailor our marketing to that segment that allowed us to grow our business significantly.

What was amazing to me was that comment cards were an underused customer service channel that merely provided us with good vibes from the comments received. We had 20 years of cards stored that I was thankful were not discarded. Not until I began to analyze the comments did I learn about the untapped potential customers and other important information that we could use to change and improve our product and delivery.

Jump ahead 40 years to today and the change and increase in customer service channels is daunting and sometimes overwhelming. The reason for my historical comparison is to show the fact that it is critical to monitor and analyze the communication channels because valuable information is there for the taking.

The challenge is to stay ahead of the technology curve and formulate a strategy to handle what I have come to call Multi-Source Customer Service. The customer now has multiple ways of communicating and researching your business. While the traditional channels of personal contact are still in place, and matter, the Internet and mobile communications have changed the game.

In the last year, mobile has become the tool of choice to access the Internet. Because of this, businesses of all sizes are playing catch-up in this revolutionary environment. Not only does everything your company does on the Internet need to become mobile-friendly, you also need to be able to handle the multiple ways in which a person can reach out to you for information.

This surge to mobile has made it easier for potential customers to reach out to you at any time; and because they are utilizing their mobile device they often expect an immediate response.

For example, Facebook now keeps track of and tells you how well you are doing concerning how quickly you respond to notifications. Their ploy is simple; the tactic keeps you coming back to your pages to keep up with any activity, which in itself creates an activity for Facebook.

Before we consider the number of platforms available for communication to a local company or division of a national company, let's look again at the basic facts about the surge in mobile. More than 50% of all searches are now done on mobile devices. More searches are for stores or things in a local area.

Most people now plan and expect to do some of their work on their mobile device. No one says that it is easy, but this allows the opportunity for you to build trust and rapport with your customers. Again the challenge for you is to strategize for the fact that customers will reach out to you on multiple platforms at the same time. They also monitor their favorite platforms and see how well you follow up to comments and questions from others. In many cases, you are on public view and your timely action and response time goes a long way to facilitate trust and authority.

In the marketplace today, those who embrace the opportunities to cover all the bases when it comes to customer service more often than not become the dominant player. I always get motivated when a business person says that they don't do Facebook, or their website does not help their business.

Multiple-Source Platforms

So what are some of the multiple-source platforms that are available to your customers for communication with your company?

- Websites
- Telephone
- Mobile Apps
- Email
- Text messages
- Facebook
- Facebook Messenger
- Facebook Groups
- Twitter
- LinkedIn
- Instagram
- Pinterest
- Podcasts
- Webinars
- YouTube
- Live Streams (Periscope/Meerkat/Blab)
- Sales Representatives
- Blogs and Comment Threads
- Newsletters

Multi-Source Strategy

Typical marketing practices today require utilization of all or most of these platforms to reach potential customers. So it is not hard to see why a monitoring and follow-up strategy is critical to staying on top of the potential communications generated by a company's marketing efforts.

It is said that it takes up to twelve interactions to make a sale or gain a customer's trust to initiate a sale. This Multiple Source Customer Service presents you with a great opportunity to build trust and rapport with customers. With multi-source customer service, you can cover all the information and questions that a prospect needs to make a purchase decision by addressing the points over multiple platforms.

When you approach the customer with a multi-source personal manner, you can figure that a sale will result if your customer gains the following trust and belief feelings.

- If they can trust you as a person.
- If you can develop a friendly and caring rapport.
- If you can demonstrate value without a firm agenda.
- If you can educate them with enough information for them to ask questions.
- If you can let them come to the conclusion that your product and service is best for them.
- If you can make them feel that they could walk away with no hard feelings or pressure.
- If you can make them feel that your customer service, follow-up, and training, if necessary, will always have them feeling secure with their decision.

You simply cannot manufacture all the trust that is needed for a sale in one sitting, but you can move up the trust ladder by quickly and efficiently managing the multi-source channels that they use and trust. Just like us, customers need to be educated in a way that allows them to be comfortable and make an intelligent business decision.

This multi-source process positions you as an expert and authority to your prospects on why they need your product or services. This action plan turns the sales process into an intelligent and proactive business decision instead of caving into another sales pitch. In many cases, the customer will become an ambassador for your success.

Implementation

So the question everyone asks is: how and when should I start the multi-source customer service process? It is easier for some businesses than others because of the product or service offered.

If the product is a specialty product, all customer service communication can be funneled to a specific person or department for facilitation. For others with a more diverse business, one person may need to wear multiple hats or have multiple people involved.

The challenge to both types of businesses is the fact that the questions are presented covering several areas of the business on each of the multi-source platforms. So depending on the type of business one person needs to handle the necessary communication or serve as a gate-keeper to bring the necessary people into the process to resolve the questions, the important thing is to start.

You don't need to address all of the potential platforms immediately, but you need to pick one or two and learn the processes and get comfortable facilitating the communication. You want to inform your customers that you are available to address their questions about your product.

A good way to do this is by answering frequently-asked questions about your products, which will often lead to other questions. Once you are comfortable with the process, you can add additional platforms or have someone else monitor other platforms.

One thing we found interesting as we continued to develop our multi-source customer service was that when we added another platform we would discover people in some cases already discussing or following our product. We just needed to start or join the interaction that always has proved beneficial for sales development.

One tool that we have found to be very helpful in the entire process is www.mention.com, which is a site where you receive a notification when anyone on the Internet mentions you, your band, or any other keyword you wish to follow. Mention is very helpful for monitoring activity on the Internet that you would potentially miss or overlook.

Certification Case Study

Probably a good way to provide an example of the multi-source customer service model is to give you a case study as to how this style of customer service and other tools discussed in this book propelled my business from a moderate six figures to seven figures in a matter of months with an on-track goal to reach five million dollars in sales in the next three years.

In 2007, I started a new business working with a high-powered pulsed electro-magnetic therapy device (PEMF) providing therapy to racehorses and performance horses around the country. I was already working in the horse industry selling therapy devices; but with this new device, which we branded as Magna Wave, I was providing the therapy treatments.

My providing the treatments was an obstacle because I was known around the country as an equipment salesperson and not a therapist. Consequently, some people felt that I did not have the qualifications to be a therapist. I did have a secondary college degree in the areas of physiology, anatomy and pathology; so my one-on-one customer service challenge became the one-on-one discussions about my education as a basis for my understanding and providing the therapy.

While that story helped the cause, the real catalyst for the business growth was that the therapy worked. In the beginning, I was a "crazy guy" pulling around this new therapy machine. Then I became "Dr. Voodoo" with this weird machine that did seem to work. Then I became the guy that veterinarians considered competition, and it must be potentially harmful or at best illegal.

The therapy became so popular that the veterinary community, for the most part, embraced it. At this point, most of the customer service discussions were face-to-face or on the phone. We had a basic web presence, but we did not have the traffic for any measurable contact or customer service through the site.

The growth at this point was a result of direct sales and contact with my potential customers. The methods worked, but I soon learned that I needed to connect with my customers from all over the country in a timely and efficient manner. So I engaged the Internet and the burgeoning social media outlets, and that is when things got messy.

There was so much to learn; and when I would learn what to do it would change, and I found myself starting again. I was drowning in a pool of technical information and strategies from everybody and their brother dealing with online marketing strategies. I found myself buying a product, starting to learn it, and then a week later someone had the next best thing, and I would jump in and start again.

My wife called it acting like a squirrel or what many call the "shiny object syndrome." In 2011, I once again purchased a new marketing product and embarked on the learning and implementation path. The difference this time was that there was a community that I could interact with for questions, support and implementable ideas on how to use the products specifically for the benefit of my company.

This was when I started to grasp the multi-source customer service model. The community became a mastermind where we could all grow and learn from each other which was very helpful. I strongly recommend that you find a mastermind group to become your sounding board for new ideas and support as you expand your customer service and Internet activities for your business.

For the first five years, my wife and I traveled the country in a motorhome, providing treatments. We were starting to do well; and as you might suspect, people began inquiring about purchasing machines to provide the therapy. I did not know where this would go, but I began selling the machines and training the new practitioners. It seemed that wherever we would travel, we would find someone wanting to purchase the equipment and begin working with their customers.

Training was not an issue because I was there treating horses in a way that provided the perfect way to train the new machine owners. Over the next three years, we grew to nearly 100 practitioners around the country, and I had to quit treating so as to not compete with the new practitioners. As you can imagine, the customer service at that point was still pretty much face-to-face and handled entirely by me as I was still pretty much a one-man show.

By this time our business revenue had grown to the mid- to upper-six-figures, and it seemed to plateau there for three years. I knew that I needed to beef up the training, and I wanted to offer training and certification as part of the program. I worked with several different platforms, but I just could not get the system going. The work and time involved seemed insurmountable.

I was actively working the Internet and social networks to grow the business because we learned that our primary customers, horsemen and horsewomen, were active on sites like Facebook. In

2010, we discovered that almost 90% of our business was in some manner moving through Facebook. Because of this we were able to sell the RV and return to Louisville and travel less.

Customer service was originating and being handled through Facebook, LinkedIn, and our website. It was late 2011 when I discovered the TPNI Engage marketing system. TPNI Engage provided an email and text auto-responder system and list building, which I desperately needed for customer service and follow-up.

I bought into the system to use it to market our products, our practitioners, and also use it for other businesses. The marketing for other businesses was a mistake because it took my focus away from Magna Wave. While at a TPNI Engage event, I was sitting in a gathering of people and I was discussing my need for a certification program, when one member of the group looked at me and said, "You can build the program within TPNI Engage; just duplicate the way they do it." I was in awe, Could it be that easy?

Within a week of my returning home from the event, the basis of my certification program was in place. The next thing I had to do was work out the logistics of promotional videos, recording the webinars, editing, hosting, SEO, and a myriad of other details.

Ultimately, I sought out the help of my mastermind group for guidance on each step of the way in producing the Magna Wave certification program. This group suggested what programs to use and in most cases helped me avoid learning curves in order to get quick implementation.

The bones were in place in two weeks, and the program launched within four weeks; and the live webinar classes were completed, recorded and edited within ten weeks. The program has been running for the past three years. I am now in the process of redoing the program and adding modules for humans and small animals. So the question is, how did the program affect the business?

The impact was immediate and dramatic. Over the first 30 to 60 days sales were up 40% and the driving force was the certification process. Some racing jurisdictions require the certification for access to the grounds with our type of device. We became the experts in the field, and our credibility and respect increased proportionately.

This momentum drove the business to seven figures, and we are well on our way to doubling our sales with the goal of reaching the mid-seven figures within the next five years. With sales tripling within two years, customer service became the focal point of our customer interaction. The staff grew from my wife and me to five, not including three commissioned sales representatives.

Our marketing has included every platform covered earlier, and the staff provides the multi-source customer service with each person covering specific areas. The multi-source customer service model is our principle tool for working with our customers including sales, training, certification, websites, practitioner business development, and training our practitioners to implement the multi-source system.

I continue to meet with my mastermind group weekly, and I ask questions about what I am currently working to accomplish. The answers I receive continue to give me direction and cut implementation time in half or more. You, too, can benefit from this brain trust of experts in the ever-changing world of Internet and offline marketing.

You cannot ask and spend the time, or you can ask and save time and make more money. My accountant used to tell me it is not how fast you find a hole, it's how fast you fill it. Make superior customer service your priority and you will not have as many holes to fill.

Contact Pat Ziemer
www.MagnaWavePEMF.com
PatZiemer@MagnaWavePEMF.com
www.facebook.com/magnawave
http://www.MWMediaDesign.com

Bonus Material
For a free 30-minute Multi-Source strategy call ($750.00 value) visit http://www.MultiSourceStrategy.com.

Biography
Pat Ziemer is the owner of Magna Wave. The company's therapy devices are used extensively on racehorses, performance horses, and professional athletes. Five recent Kentucky Derby winners and

numerous world champions in many horse disciplines utilize the therapy regularly. In 2007, Pat acquired the rights to the PEMF device, repackaged it, branded it as Magna Wave and hit the road marketing the Magna Wave brand.

Since 2007 Pat has placed over 600 Magna Wave devices into the market for private and professional use, primarily in the equine marketplace. The company is now moving into the areas of human and small animal therapy.

Chapter 8: Scaling Customer Engagement

How a Virtual Summit Can Help You Get Your Brand Message in Front of Thousands of Your Ideal Customers at the Same Time

by Michael Alf

Imagine your business is attracting 12,491 of your ideal potential customers to a three-day event. Of those 12,491 participants, 2,756 are buying at the event and are becoming customers. Furthermore, imagine you have a high level of live engagement where participants are asking various questions, sharing their challenges and problems and responding in different ways to the questions you are asking.

Such an event makes both the new customers and all the active participants ambassadors for your business who are potentially spreading the word and sharing their experiences.

All of this is possible with a Virtual Summit.

So What Exactly Is a Virtual Summit?

A Virtual Summit is an event, or conference, or show that utilizes modern digital technologies and the Internet to make the content, the speakers, the audio and video available remotely on various devices like computers, laptops, tablets and smartphones.

There are different models of Virtual Summits. They can be live, or recorded, or mixed. They can last for one day, three days, two weeks, or even more. There can be one speaker, a few speakers – in sequence or in parallel – or there can be a large number of speakers.

Virtual Summits have been around for a few years but they are now becoming more and more popular – especially in the United States, but also in other parts of the world. You might have already participated in a summit or you might have seen and have been invited to a summit. If the subject is completely new to you, please read on to learn how to get started with a virtual summit for your business.

Whenever a new tool or a new way of doing something comes up, people develop reasons why this is not going to work. So I would like to begin by busting three myths about Virtual Summits which you might have heard, or you might know somebody who believes they are true.

3 Myths about Virtual Summits

1. Virtual Summits No Longer Work

The concept of Virtual Summits is not very old, but they have been around for a few years; so more and more people are hearing about the summits – both the successful ones and the less successful summits.

This created a myth that Virtual Summits don't work anymore. People are sick and tired of them.

Nothing could be further from the truth.

Think about the following. Real-world summits, events and fairs have always been around. It's the place where you learn from experts, get up-to-date information about trends in your industry, connect with people, and get motivated and inspired.

One of the challenges is obviously the cost of such events – for the organizers and also the attendants, especially when they have to cover travel and accommodations cost.

Still, events keep their popularity.

I even think they are more relevant than ever. The main reason for this is the fast-changing world. It's definitely important to stay up-to-date, to learn what is coming next, and to understand how to implement things into your life or your business.

That's where Virtual Summits come in. They provide a similar experience, learning from experts and getting inspired. They don't carry the large price tag of the physical equivalents. They also provide a high level of flexibility, because during a three-day event you can pick and choose what you are really interested in and you can still follow your work. Or you can watch sessions at a later stage when you have some more spare time.

The area where Virtual Summits are probably falling short a bit is the connection between people. Depending on the set-up, there are opportunities to connect and engage with other participants and with speakers but it's not face to face. In our summits, we are exploring and testing various ways and approaches to see what works best.

So Virtual Summits do work and I believe they are here to stay.

2. No Interaction

As mentioned previously, another major concern is that there is limited interaction between participants and also with the speakers.

I acknowledge that you cannot sit around a table with other participants and look them in the eye.

But we have used a number of powerful mechanics and tools to foster interaction on a different level. You can create a very interactive and dynamic environment encouraging participants to contribute and to ask questions. And because it's largely anonymous there might be more openness from participants in sharing their problems and challenges.

Another very powerful result and outcome we found was the engagement and connection between the speakers. Because you can organize global events, it's easier to connect speakers who would usually not or rarely get together. And the Virtual Summit provides a common goal to work towards.

In summary I would say that you can orchestrate interaction for summits, but you also might consider how to combine both modi operandi – the physical event and the virtual event.

3. You Cannot Reach the Audience

Another concern I hear regularly is that it's hard to reach the audience and get them to join the summit. Yes, I agree the marketplace is crowded and there is lots of noise. But consider the following.

When you are a consumer company it's usually very hard to connect with your end customers. Today you might do a fair bit of social media but you are looking for more ways. Then a Virtual Summit is a great way to achieve this outcome.

And when you haven't done a lot to really engage with your end customers it's even more relevant and provides a way to directly connect with your audience.

With regard to reaching the audience, I would say that today basically everybody is on social media channels like Facebook, YouTube or LinkedIn. And all those platforms offer ads you can run to your target group. When you already have a strong Facebook following but the organic posts don't have a good reach, you can target your own Facebook fans with specific ads motivating them to join the summit. Combining this with great speakers increases the probability that people are signing up for your Virtual Summit.

Four Ways to Get Started with Creating a Virtual Summit

Now that we have unseated a number of myths about Virtual Summits, I would like to give you four steps that you could take to get started with your Virtual Summit.

Step 1. What Is a Potential Virtual Summit (Theme) for Your Business?

The first phase of a Virtual Summit is the planning phase; and you can read more about that in my book which you can download as a bonus. One of the first things is to consider the theme of your summit. What is the summit about? What is the big message of the summit? For example we ran one summit which was called "Thermie Living Lifestyle Summit." While the topic – lifestyle – was a little broad, the audience (owners of a specific kitchen appliance) was really targeted. And as a result we got great opt-in rates and conversion rates.

So think about your business and what kind of summit you could offer. For example, if you are in the supplement business you could run a Virtual Summit on "How to Become Summer-Ready." And you could use your ambassadors as speakers. In the presentations, the speakers could talk about how they used certain supplements to become fit and healthy and reach their ideal weight in combination with exercise and nutrition. I am not giving any medical advice here.

The next element of the theme is the title of your summit. Some of the examples of summits we have run include: Thermie Living Lifestyle Summit, Ultimate Man Summit, Freedom Business Summit, Entrepreneurial Executive Summit.

The title should be compelling and should be very specific regarding what the summit is about and who the audience is for the summit.

Step 2. What Are Potential Speakers for Your Summit?

Once you are clear about the theme of the summit you can focus on the speakers. Obviously the speakers are the key ingredient for a great summit, so choose wisely.

When you already have links and connections to celebrities in your market you could ask as speakers, great! But usually you don't necessarily have that and instead you might have some ideas for the right speakers. When brainstorming your speaker list, don't start small but start with the ideal candidates and speakers. In my book, *The Virtual Summit Formula*, I talk about the concept of an anchor speaker which is somebody who is very high caliber, very visible or well known, who can attract both other speakers and a great audience.

Let's say you want to run a retail summit. You could try to get the CEO of Walmart as the anchor speaker. That's the level I suggest to think of speakers.

The number of speakers really depends upon your model and the duration of the summit. You can get started with five speakers who are presenting on one day. Or you can have 10 speakers over two or three days ... or even stretch it out over seven days. But you can also go really big and have 20 speakers and more and "jam-pack" your Virtual Summit with highlights and speakers.

The risk of having too many speakers is that it gets overwhelming for the audience. And this might decrease the interaction and even participation. So balancing the intent of adding value to the audience with a digestible amount of content is the key requirement here.

I would suggest when you do your first summit, plan for four to five days and have between two to three speakers per day. That results in 8 to 15 speakers overall and is still manageable. This is particularly true when you run the Virtual Summit without external help.

Step 3. Potential Models

Now that you have a great list of speakers you can approach, you need to consider which Virtual Summit model you are applying.

One key differentiation you can make is between "stretched summit" and "condensed summit." Let's look into it in more detail.

A stretched summit is a summit that spans over a longer period (it is stretched in terms of duration). The idea behind this is that you "drip-feed" content to the audience. This way the content does not become overwhelming. The audience has one presentation per day and can watch and listen whenever they find the time. Often presentations are up to one hour so you need to find one hour of time to consume the daily content. That is usually feasible for an interested audience.

So how far should you stretch the summit out? I have seen summits running over weeks, but personally I wouldn't recommend this. The momentum goes away and people get bored by it. I suggest you pick a duration of not more than two weeks. And if you identified more than 15 speakers in step 2 you could offer two speakers at the weekends where people have generally more time. One of our summits went via two weeks and we had a total of 19 speakers during those 15 days.

Alternatively you could have a "condensed" summit. The most condensed version is a one-day summit with up to 10 speakers. This can become very intense in terms of preparation but also execution. And when you run this one-day event/summit live it is even more critical to have an experienced team who has done this kind of summit before.

A less-intensive version of the condensed summit is a two-day event with, for example, six speakers per day. Especially when your focus is on one time zone, you can mimic a real summit with a morning, a lunch break, and an afternoon event. That makes it easier to manage and plan for the engagement during the summit.

That way you can pack 12 speakers into two days. This is most likely done on a weekend or maybe Friday/Saturday like a classical physical summit. Otherwise it gets too challenging for your audience to attend.

And in between those two models you can vary, depending on your circumstances, speakers, topics, etc.

Now that you have a model you can get started with the preparation and execution phase.

Step 4. Learn How to Run a Virtual Summit or Find Somebody Who Can Help

A lot of the preparation is done with the previous three steps. Of course there is a lot more to talk about but this gives you a great start in creating your own Virtual Summit.

To move forward from here you or your team need to learn how to effectively run those Virtual Summits. As you can imagine, there is a lot to consider and plan for so it does become a project in its own right. As the reader of this book, I would like to give you my book, The Virtual Summit Formula, which is an international #1 best seller, as a bonus. In the book I present the 7-stage *Virtual Summit Formula* which I break down into 20 single steps. Reading this book will help you or your team to wrap your head around the execution phase of a summit.

Please click here to download the book. http://tiny.cc/csuite.

With this book you can map out the process and identify where you have gaps in your organization. You might have most of the capabilities already and just need to appoint a good project manager to execute the whole summit.

Or you might come to the conclusion that there are a few missing pieces and systems. Then the guide will help you to close those. Or you can, of course, reach out and get help.

I strongly believe Virtual Summits are a very powerful tool for many businesses. They are flexible and will evolve over time as the technology changes; but they offer a level of interaction with your customers that hardly anything else can provide. So that's why I would like to close this chapter with the following quote.

"Each year I host a leadership summit in my district, and my biggest advice to young people is get experience. Get your foot in the door." – **Aaron Schock**

So get your foot in the door and get started with your first Virtual Summit for your business!

Contact Michael Alf

michael@virtualsummitformula.com
https://www.linkedin.com/in/michaelalfmel

Bonus Material

Download the free PDF version of Michael's #1 best-selling book, *The Virtual Summit Formula*, which describes the 7-stage virtual summit process at http://tiny.cc/csuite.

Biography

After a global senior executive career, Michael Alf decided to start his own business. He is founder of the Virtual Summit Formula, author of multiple international #1 best-selling books, who also helps clients create and publish books to help them with their positioning in the marketplace.

His specialty is virtual summits that attract hundreds and thousands of participants, grow and elevate a business, and create significant exposure in the marketplace. With summits like Thermie Living Lifestyle Summit, Freedom Business Summit, Ultimate Man Summit, Entrepreneurial Executive Summit or the Healthy Weight Summit, Michael has developed multiple approaches and a wealth of experience around virtual summits.

Before his entrepreneurial journey, Michael was a senior executive with extensive experience in global, regional and local roles in IT leadership, consulting, transformation, business development and general management within the services business.

He has had broad exposure to retail, energy, utilities and FMCG, with particular strength in logistics, working across all modes from mail, express, logistics, freight, rail, ports and corporate services (procurement, HR and finance). He started his career with the Federal Armed Forces in Germany attaining the rank of Captain.

Chapter 9: Elevating and Engaging Your Brand to the Connected Customer

The Five Key Strategies of Content Marketing for Success

by Stephen Saber, M.B.A.

Content marketing has received a lot of buzz and hype over the past couple of years as it grows in momentum; and for good reason. As the next generation of consumer comes into the marketplace, the need for companies to compete on a whole new level has become even more obvious and critical. There is a commonly-used statistic from a 2012 study by **SiriusDecisions** that is becoming more relevant every day – that *70% of the buying decision is made prior to meeting the customer.*

That buying decision is being influenced first and foremost through research and education online by consumers who are in the buying cycle. In the Massachusetts area there used to be a retail company named Syms that said: "An educated consumer is our best customer."

In the world of online content and social media, "An educated consumer is every customer."

• Car buyers are coming into dealerships knowing the car they want, whether it is in the inventory, what the sticker price is, what options they want, and who is selling it for how much.

• Real estate buyers are now able to look online at every house that is for sale, figure out which they want to look at, understand the relative prices of comps in the area, and what has sold recently for what prices.

•   B2B product buyers are coming to meetings with knowledge about whose products are offered, what features they are providing, what the customer feedback has been, and how the product is being implemented.

Content marketing is about influencing the 70% by reaching the customer with educational and relevant content about the industry, the marketplace, the challenges and solutions, and ultimately your brand. Content marketing breaks down into five parts – Content Creation, Content Curation, Content Distribution, Content Syndication, and Analytics. To understand effective content marketing, it is critical to understand these five components and how they fit together.

Before beginning, it is important to understand one concept that is becoming critical in content marketing programs – the development of your own digital publication.

The Digital Publication

American Express was an early adopter in this phenomenon of the digital publication when they launched Open Forum – a site for small business owners. Open Forum is not about American Express. Instead, it is about the small business owner and the struggles that he/she fights every day. While powered by American Express, the site is dedicated to the needs of the small business owner.

To do this, American Express recruited a series of respected bloggers and authors to be contributors to the site, lending their expertise to the efforts – and thus ultimately supporting the notion that American Express cared about the small business owner.

Citrix did the same thing with Workshifting.com – reaching out to the remote employee, someone working outside the office, with content relevant to them.

A clear reason a digital publication is so important is that it allows you not to "outsource your customer." It is the desire of every social media platform provider to own the customer database. Their business model is predicated on organizations building their communities on their platform and allowing the site to own the customer database.

The smart companies are building publication sites and using the social media platforms as drivers to bring prospects, consumers, and customers to the sites, and "taking back their databases."

The digital publication movement is similar to what happened in the event industry 10-15 years ago. At one time, all trade shows and conferences were run by associations or by for-profit producers. Slowly at first and then faster recently, companies began to run their own events and turn those events from being focused on them to being industry-focused programs. The same phenomenon is happening online.

Content Creation

According to many organizations, the number one issue stopping companies from implementing content marketing programs is that it is too difficult to create content. Existing staff usually does not have the time to create content and the company may not have the resources necessary to do so. The reality, in fact, could not be further from the truth.

Companies have a plethora of content about their industry and their organization and products and services at their fingertips – most of which goes unused and un-consumed. The key to a successful content creation effort is to simplify the efforts of content creation to take it from a daunting task that seems to be overwhelming and impossible to become part of the everyday culture of the organization. And the key to this is to start with video.

Think about a simple series of questions. If someone were asked to write a 500-word e-book or document, the typical reaction would be: "I don't have the time to make that happen." However, if asked, "Do you have the time for a 20-minute phone call?" – most would make the time. Now, asked if that phone call could be on video, most would respond positively.

Successful content creation efforts often begin with video to capture the main content. From there, a multi-channel marketing effort can be created. Blog posts can be written. Podcasts can be created. E-books can be created. And video marketing snippets can be created. With an hour's worth of video, a month's worth of content can be created.

But often, the question asked is: "What is the topic?" The answer is: the topic that will answer the question of your buyer. In other words, "What keeps them up at night?" By generating content related to the needs of the customer, companies are reaching that 70% of the buying decision and ultimately affecting outcomes.

It is often important to look at what content the company currently has and how that can be brought to the forefront. Have white papers been created that are not being read? Have how-to tutorials been created that are not utilized? One of the easiest ways to create content is to find these "content nuggets" and bring them to life with video and a multi-channel content effort.

For every content creation effort, a key ingredient is structure. In video, this is called a "run-down." A run-down is a template layout that outlines how the content will be created based on how it will be utilized after creation. The structure provides two key ingredients: (1) for the content creator it creates an outline he/she can follow which makes the content creation effort concrete instead of being vague and wide open; and (2) it creates a model for the content to ensure that it fits within the plan for marketing post creation.

Content Curation

An often-overlooked opportunity for marketers in content marketing efforts is the power of content curation. Content curation is the process whereby a marketer identifies and "tags" and "shares" articles of interest as part of a marketing effort.

Let's break it down. People surf the web all of the time. The vast amount of content that anyone is expected to consume to stay "abreast" of the happenings in their industry segment is overwhelming and in many ways impossible to stay up-to-date with. To that end, a company's content marketing efforts related to content curation aim to help prospects and customers fight through the noise.

The "offer" to the community and prospects is as follows: "Instead of being concerned with reading through and filtering through the vast amount of content out there, we will do it for you and highlight the key articles of interest." In doing so, the content marketer accomplishes three key goals:

1.   Provide valuable content to your prospects to stay "top of mind" (i.e., relevant and memorable) and relevant.

2.   Establish your organization as a "thought leader" in your space by expressing that your organization is the organization to turn to in order to know what is important.

3.   Create content without much effort and interruption in people's daily workflow.

As previously discussed, a key factor in NOT implementing content marketing efforts is the impression that organizations do not have the resources to create content. To that end, content curation is the solution to this question. By asking key team members to simply "highlight" or "flag" the articles that they come across that they deem worth reading and sharing – reading that they are probably doing anyway in the ordinary course of their business – content marketing teams can get access to content marketing resources with little or no interruption in the workflow of team members.

Content Distribution

All content marketing efforts are based on the ability to use content to reach out to customers and prospects. To that end, a good content marketing plan requires a strong base of content distribution. The key components of this plan rely on: Cadence, Content Assets, and Channels.

Cadence refers to the creation and implementation of a "content calendar" which identifies and outlines the timing and schedule of content interactions. Online consumers have grown to develop inherent expectations of when to expect and when to consume content from channels they trust.

When content marketing efforts fail, oftentimes it is because the delivery of content follow an unscheduled calendar of distribution and therefore the "relationship" that the content marketer hopes to develop with the prospect never gets established. To that end, establishing a calendar with a clear periodic schedule that fits and is appropriate for the prospect base is critical in building and developing that relationship.

In addition, as the content marketing programs are put into production, it is important that content marketers make the prospect aware of the timing, develop those expectations, and cement those relationships.

"Content channels" refers to the ways that content marketers will reach the prospect. In particular, it is important to segment beyond just thinking of email, alerts, video, SMS, social channels, and podcasts, and to think deeper of the type of communication that will work within this channel.

For instance, in looking at email as a channel, there are at least three types of emails to consider. The first is the basic alert email with a single piece of content highlighted and distributed. The second is a newsletter which outlines several pieces of content that fit together as a series of related content assets.

The third is a variation of the newsletter – something referred to as a "Top 5" – which is a newsletter that is expected to be read very quickly which highlights five pieces of content that should be / can be consumed – but in essence is a distribution mechanism for easy reading and "top of mind" value. The same breakdown can be and should be looked at for each of the aforementioned channels.

With the plan for distribution, it becomes critical to look at which content assets fit with which channels. Some assets, like curated content, fit into one channel better than another channel. For instance, in the above example, curated content is a perfect fit for the "Top 5" email campaign whereas video assets and created assets are more appropriate for a newsletter campaign.

Likewise, in social outreach the content that works and is appropriate for a Twitter campaign differs from that which is appropriate for a Facebook campaign which differs from a LinkedIn campaign.

Together, Cadence / Content Assets / and Channels make up a content distribution plan that will reach the prospects, develop and deepen relationships, and build trust in affecting the 70% decision process of the consumer.

Content Syndication

Unlike content distribution, which refers to connecting to the channels that the content marketer "owns" and "manages," content syndication refers to reaching out to channels that the content marketer does not own but can access. In marketing worlds, the references are to "owned media," "earned media," and "paid media." Content distribution programs are efforts that focus on the "owned media" – channels that the content marketer controls. Content syndication programs are efforts that focus on "earned media" and "paid media."

The power of creating valuable content is the opportunity to reach "earned media" outlets that might previously have been unavailable to organizations. While media organizations would have shunned outreach from organizations and tried to turn those into "paid" opportunities, if an organization delivers quality, valuable, insightful content, media organizations are often thirsty for this type of content to provide to its database.

In many ways, content syndication's goal is to capture access to other organizations' databases by providing content they are wanting and willing to share. As an example, if an organization were to just ask a thought leader with many followers for access to their databases, they would be met with either a price tag or with a "no." However, if that thought leader were invited to participate in a content creation effort with the organization and then provided with that content asset to share, the likelihood of that content being shared is much higher.

In thinking about "paid media," the key aspect of content syndication comes back to the idea of reaching the 70% research happening before the buying decision. Organizations are often taking the "easy way out" when it comes to paid advertising and online advertising – buying ads and pointing them back to the organization's website. "Paid media" programs with content marketing change this model by inserting valuable content in the middle of that relationship.

Instead of ads pointing to a website and an offer, these efforts point those ads to valuable content which in turn references and connects the organization. This content lives in the digital publication which references and is powered by the organization, thereby creating and establishing that thought leader position and affecting that 70%.

Analytics

With any content marketing program, there will be a lot of trial and error. It is critical that the organization is "agile" in its marketing programs – measuring along the way and adjusting the programs and plans in real-time as results are recorded. As personas are developed and distribution and syndication plans implemented, the results in terms of content consumption, content types, channels, conversions, and lead scoring will determine and highlight what is working and what needs to be adjusted.

As an example, a recent content marketing program began with a live web TV series with monthly live programming. It was thought that the consumers would want and value the live interaction because the thought leaders on the live programs were typically unavailable to the prospects and communities.

Soon, based on analytics such as content consumption viewership and length of viewing, it became evident that the content was not being consumed live but instead being consumed later and on demand – typically in the evening and weekends. To that end, the content marketing program was adjusted. Live programming was eliminated and more on-demand content was added.

Another interesting thing that came out was the strong pull of Facebook for syndication. It was originally assumed that since the audience was typically a middle-aged male, the reach of Facebook would be minimal at best and therefore little budget was applied. When it was determined that Facebook was a strong tool for content syndication – even to this demographic – budgets were adjusted and plans changed.

Conclusion

In summary, a content marketing plan works to reach the consumer prior to making the buy decision. As it is widely known, 70% of the buying decision is made prior to connecting with the prospect. To that end, content marketing will affect that 70% while also providing valuable content in an education-marketing effort.

By combining this effort with a content distribution and content syndication plan, a content marketer can reach prospects where they want to be reached, when they want to connect, through the channels they want to communicate, and with the content they want to consume. In doing so, organizations create and establish thought leadership, create market and brand positioning, and ultimately generate marketing and sales-qualified leads.

Contact Stephen Saber

http://www.linkedin.com/in/ssaber
http://www.stephensaber.com
http://www.facebook.com/Stephensaber
http://twitter.com/stephensaber

Bonus Material

Check out Stephen's free videos, "Marketing Unwrapped," at http://tpniuniversity.tpni.com.

Biography

Stephen Saber is currently the CEO of The Pulse Network (OTCBB: TPNI). The Pulse Network provides a cloud-based platform focused on content marketing and event solutions. The company helps clients ranging from Fortune 500 companies to small and mid-size companies boost awareness, drive lead generation, and enhance client engagement through content marketing, campaign management and event registration with a social and digital backbone.

Stephen was formerly president of CrossTech Partners and CEO of New Marketing Labs, which merged with The Pulse Network in the spring of 2011. Earlier in his career he was a managing director at Cambridge Technology Partners (CTP) – one of the fastest-growing public IT services companies. CTP became the leading IT consulting and systems integration firm focused on the deployment of client-server-based business applications for Fortune 500 clients. Stephen has played a leading advisory role in major M&A transactions ranging from $30M to $450M in Digital Media and IT. Stephen received his M.B.A. from Harvard Business School and B.A. from Harvard University.

Chapter 10: Get Off Your Assets! Innovate Now

7 Monetization Strategies to Convert Your Existing Content into Cash

by Niki Faldemolaei

It has never been as easy and inexpensive to produce and distribute your own content than right now. With the rapid growth of more than seven billion active cellular mobile accounts, and 67% of buyers initiating their purchases via smartphone, it is imperative that companies innovate to adopt digital strategies into their marketing and sales mix.

Senior executives are adopting the mindset of creating a technically-competitive organization; but when it comes to walking the talk, many fall short on actually taking action. More and more prospects and hiring agencies are vetting a brand by the presence (or absence) of the C-level executives' social influence score. Their ability to demonstrate that they truly understand the importance of evolving digital trends can directly affect how well they attract and retain key customers and employees.

To attract the best Chief Marketing Officer, as an example, companies are best served when executives consider the CMO to be like an air traffic controller, often tracking changes in an industry before others. They provide a context for those who make decisions in an organization. They carefully watch and test analytics of their messaging to see how prospects and customers react and can intelligently shift a direction or bulk-up on resources where needed to get the best result. The CMO is fast becoming considered a revenue generator as opposed to a cost center.

It is no longer sufficient to rely on the typical C-suite with your standard roles of CEO-COO-CIO-CMO-CTO. As these roles overlap with technology dynamically changing each one, a new role is emerging, the Chief Digital Officer, CDO, who holds a board-level, strategic mandate between that of the CEO and other CXOs or silos of an organization. It is not a silo unto itself.

Because marketing technology is so quick to change, it can be difficult to hire or retain the perfect mix of talent. Sixty-two percent of companies outsource all or part of their digital marketing, mainly the most difficult types. Outsourcing supplements internal skills to improve performance.

Marketing technology experts are a new breed of talent who actively test the latest technology platforms and channels of distribution through each of their clients. Most become certified in multiple platforms, giving them an unfair advantage over the old school consulting firms.

It is not unusual to find teams of highly-skilled, former executives who have adopted digital marketing as their new playing field. They make incredible outsourcing candidates for organizations who are not able to hire teams, and can often be covered under additional budget line items such as education, research and/or technology.

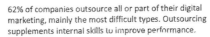

62% of companies outsource all or part of their digital marketing, mainly the most difficult types. Outsourcing supplements internal skills to improve performance.

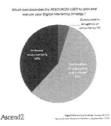

Ascend2

Let's do an exercise for a minute and reframe what you are doing in your business. Most companies produce far more content than they ever utilize. From white papers and speeches to blog posts and market research, any organization can digitize a great deal of relevant data that can be repurposed into news bytes and saleable assets.

American Express was wildly successful using Facebook to post images and videos, to the tune of receiving five million "likes" on their business page. What they discovered is that they had archives of data that was sitting, unused. They repurposed this content and created an "American Express Milestones" series of posts that spanned the lifetime of their company founded in 1890. Such a collection can now be repurposed into an e-book, blog posts, LinkedIn discussion groups, or even turned into videos.

IBM, Target, and Four Seasons are notable for using a combination of curated and created content in virtually every format under the sun, including:

- Blogs
- Microsites (education or finance divisions)
- Print and digital publications
- Social media conversations
- Visual content (infographics, animations)
- Podcasts
- Video (product demos, short films)
- Apps (gaming)
- User-generated content
- Multichannel experiences
- And more!

No matter what type of business you have, you are in show business – the business of showing people your skills and knowledge. You are also in the event business. Your success relies upon the events you attend or host and the people with whom you surround yourself.

When you engage with your network of influencers at a trade show, through interactive social forums or directly via your sales team, you automatically get real-time feedback to your offerings, enabling you to tweak and correct as you go. At that point, and only then, it is your engaging content that will attract the biggest brands in the world, including Amazon, Apple, Facebook, Google, LinkedIn, Twitter and

YouTube. These mega-giants will actively promote your engaging offerings, and some will even pay you to bring them your content.

The path of least resistance is the ideal way to start. Let's use New York Times best-selling author JJ Virgin as an example, who has produced a system for weight management and healthy lifestyle in California. JJ routinely speaks at conferences, hosts a healthy network show online, and sells supplements, workshops and books. She is an ideal candidate for success because she is an implementer who had hundreds of hours of content that was underutilized! It simply needed to be repurposed and launched to maximize distribution! We will visit "7 Ways to Profit" later in this chapter.

Since video and streaming are mega-trends for billions of users with smartphones and tablets, our first step with an organization is to start gathering and capturing their content with video. YouTube Live is a free service that enables us to capture their interviews live, share screens, and feature their guests in real time. With a simple adjustment, we add their existing commercials and sponsors to these live events to monetize the show.

"I learned more about my audience in a 2-hour livecast than I had in the past 10 years of marketing and growing into a successful 7-figure business!" – **Celebrity Nutrition and Fitness Expert JJ Virgin**, a four-time *NY Times* best-selling author

Our strategy is to keep our companies in motion, like JJ, tweaking something they already do (turning content into audio and video). Then we repurpose and/or add bonuses with books, CDs, DVDs and workshops as we map automated educational, marketing, and sales campaigns. We then deliver this content everywhere in every format to every device, a strategy known as multicast marketing.

For those who do not have a lot of content to repurpose, as in a start-up company, we might begin with an interview-style video capture session. Since this brand is an unknown, they might choose to leverage other people's talent and brand recognition by inviting public figures or experts to be guest interviewees.

A real-world example of a start-up success, Entrepreneur on Fire founder John Lee Dumas discovered the magic when he started interviewing successful business owners about their strategies and achievements. He started by asking well-known authors and entrepreneurs with recent business success stories to be interviewed on his show. In doing so, he leveraged their expertise and networks expanding 10 times beyond his own influence. He executed the fastest route and launched his daily drive-time podcast to build a 7-figure empire in only 13 months!

Another real-world example of early adopters of digitizing their shows is the trend where celebrities have moved from TV to online streaming. Late night host Jay Leno, anchorwoman Katie Couric, and E!'s Chelsea Handler have moved from cable TV networks to online shows.

With the onset of mobile device dominance for our attention span, there is huge growth potential for savvy companies in virtually any industry. Whether you are a doctor, CEO or financial maven, you have the opportunity to become the early-adopter of a ridiculously-inexpensive business model that is threatening to be the next disruptive technology. Next we will take a look at some creative ways to use the content from your show to achieve multicast profits.

7 Monetization Strategies to Convert Your Existing Content into Cash

It's the age of multi-channel, omni-channel, and multi-device shopping. The lines between offline and online shopping experiences are increasingly blurring:

- 44% of consumers research online and buy online
- 51% research online and visit a store to purchase
- 17% visit a store first and then purchase online
- 32% research online, visit a store to view a product, and then return online to make a purchase

1. Multicast

The strategy of creating content once, then repurposing it to reach every device, in every format, delivering content everywhere in the world is referred to as multicast marketing. Your customers want to consume your content in their preferred way, whether it is auditory, visual or kinesthetic. Creating your multi-platform content and distributing it in multicast outlets gives you an unfair advantage in reaching your target audience.

Your profit lever: No matter where your customer looks, they can now find properly-ranked content that is yours. Over 220 million buyers seek to purchase via Amazon. Over 400 million buyers seek to purchase via Apple Store. There are more than two billion tablets, three billion laptops, and seven billion smartphones on which persons shop and consume engaging content like yours. Leveraging these digital landscapes is vital to business success. Visit http://multicastprofits.com for more information.

"Globally 3.2 billion people are using the Internet at the end of 2015." – **ICT Facts & Figures 2015**

2. Livecast

Your speeches or shows can be captured via video and/or broadcast with YouTube Live for free with unlimited viewers. This digital technology is replacing analog broadcast, cable and film. You can now replace radio and TV with free delivery tools connecting to virtually any device, anytime, anywhere. Notably important is how webinars and the latest trend in Blab, Periscope and Meerkat, are capturing content real-time, to build a library of opportunities.

Your profit lever: Utilizing your show with the leverage of your guest's brand is a powerful way to engage your audience in deadline offers, live discounts, and bonuses, each pointing to new and enticing added-value offers. Product launches in the Internet marketing worlds have consistently reached million-dollar days from a single livecast event. Webinar replays, set up correctly, also prove this multi-six and seven-figure model. Visit http://multicastprofits.com for more.

3. Podcast

This is the most overlooked opportunity in online marketing. Podcasting is as simple as taking your audio, video and PDF content and distributing it to the 800-pound gorilla Apple to reach millions of buyers so they can see your content. With most new cars equipped for streaming, drive-time podcasts are an ideal form of capturing your audience for an average 26 minutes twice a day, seven days a week.

Your profit lever: Podcasters have surpassed the radio and TV talk show model and turned it into a self-sustaining business with earnings from subscriptions and/or advertising and sponsorships. When your subscribers listen to you on the run, in the car, or on headphones, you have the multi-touch intimacy of which most marketers can only dream. Visit http://multicastprofits.com for more.

As seen on

4. Bookcast

Attaining "Author Expert" status is a powerful way to position yourself as an authority in order to open doors for media interviews, speaking engagements and consulting gigs. It is as easy as taking your show content, transcribing it, and turning it into a book. The old paradigm where authors hope to make their income from book sales has taken a critical turn toward the creative.

Your profit lever: Your book is your ticket to partnerships with media events, charitable programs and corporate endorsements. Gifting your book to key account management or offering to give your book away at joint events with relevant brand names elevates your status as an expert. Leveraging these partnerships expands your reach 10x $$$ beyond a traditional book tour. You quickly earn the right to use "As seen on…," adding mega-media logos in your promotions. Visit http://multicastprofits.com for more.

5. Mobilecast

A mind-blowing seven billion mobile accounts exist (approaching the 7.3 billion world population), making the mobile delivery market the most dynamic potential for growth. Soon, texting, SMS, MMS and scanning QR codes will be standard procedure for gathering leads from live events, networking circles and online buyers. Leads build lists. Lists, when strategically executed, build assets.

Your profit lever: Since more than 67% of purchases are initiated via mobile, and sales are dependent on your list, the mobile capture of leads has a direct impact on revenue. Most Futurists will agree that mobile commerce is one of the most important trends of this time. You are in the right place at the right time to put your content in the pockets of billions. Seize it! Visit http://multicastprofits.com for more.

"By the end of 2015, there are more than 7 billion mobile cellular subscriptions, corresponding to a penetration rate of 97%, up from 738 million in 2000." **– ICT Facts & Figures 2015**

6. Socialcast

Syndication of your content is key to building your brand and your income. You can now cater to your audience on their terms, where they spend their time. You might reach a customer on Twitter or a business colleague on LinkedIn. Whether your audience is blogging or watching YouTube videos, they will find you. What this means for business is that there is a new way to target success through a social influence score.

Your profit lever: Engagement of your high-scoring, targeted audience through social sharing of bonus offers and incentives puts customers into a queue where they are fed your high-quality, meaningful content over time, to build trust, followed by the conversion to sales after three, seven, or 12 interactions with you. Visit http://multicastprofits.com for more.

"When companies such as Disney, Nike, and Microsoft are creating successful marketing efforts centered on people's social influence scores, as a

business professional, you'd better take that seriously." – **Mark Schaefer,**
author *of Return on Influence*

7. Broadcast

You may have heard the prediction that Cable is dying thanks in
part to Netflix, Hulu and Amazon. As markets shift from analog to
digital delivery, media organizations are scrambling to stay current
while their programming and operations are disrupted by the onset of
iTV, tablets and smartphones as the preferred way to watch shows.

Your profit lever: This is a perfect time for your show to be
that trend, or for you to become a consultant to celebrities, casting
directors, writers, and producers for TV/film. You may provide key
education in a specific role, or show an idea from drone pilots to
holographic education … or relationship guru to investment disruptor.
Digitizing your content and positioning yourself as an expert in your
field gives you an unfair advantage. Get there first! Visit http://
multicastprofits.com for more.

Conclusion

Since over 70% of buyers who arrive to make a purchase have
already made up their mind as to what they intend to purchase, it is
imperative that your content was key in their researched decision.
This means your content needs to be at their fingertips everywhere, in
every format, on every device, long before the sale takes place.

Global Content Marketing Trends to Watch in 2015-16

- Number of brands using content marketing continues to grow annually, particularly in emerging markets;
- B2C (Consumer) content marketing is forecast to grow faster than B2B (Business) content marketing;
- Mobile content & apps will be fastest growing of PQ's 13 content marketing (CM) channels;
- Microsoft's development of Multi-Channel Networks expected to fuel branded video growth;
- Major brands, however, monitoring changes at social nets like YouTube, which seek to share revenues;
- Sponsored market research and webinars among fastest growing B2B content channels;
- Proliferation of self-publishing sites driving growth of sponsored books – fastest growing print channel;
- Sponsored games & branded content tools to be used more to engage young demos, such as iGens;
- More global events being held to help B2B & B2C content publishers educate & sell CM to brands;
- Measurement remains challenge for brands to feel more "satisfied" with CM campaign results

 pqmedia

www.pqmedia.com

Content marketing has become more important than advertising and has disrupted the way technically-competitive companies can win the race of digital creation and consumption of marketing information.

The successful executives and brands are those who move with the trend and "hire smart"; who build a perfect mix of CXO, employee and outsourced talent to maximize the return on investment as well as stand out in the marketplace.

Notes

(1)   http://www.itu.int/en/ITU-D/Statistics/Documents/facts/ICTFactsFigures2015.pdf and https://www.cmocouncil.org/facts-stats-categories.php?view=all&category=mobile-marketing

(2)   Social Influence Score – A calculation based on an algorithm of how and where you show up in social media, blogs and press.

(3)   Social Influence – An extension of word-of-mouth marketing adding behaviors that include social media, blogs and press.

(4)   Content Editorial Statement – http://contentmarketinginstitute.com/2015/10/statement-content-marketing.

(5)   Disruptive Technology is an innovation that helps create a new market and value network, and eventually disrupts an existing market and value network, displacing an earlier technology. An example would be how Netflix and Hulu are displacing cable TV.

(6)   Read more at http://www.business2community.com/marketing/first-step-road-becoming-multi-channel-marketing expert-01177942#i4eoTikftH2So7RG.99.

(7)   http://contentmarketinginstitute.com/2015/05/content-marketing-tips/

Disclaimer

Results are not typical. We are not lawyers or CPAs and recommend you check in with your counsel when choosing to engage in this new world of marketing technology.

Contact Niki Faldemolaei

http://TempleArtsCommunications.com

http://MulticastProfits.com

https://www.linkedin.com/in/faldemolaei
https://www.facebook.com/faldemolaei
https://twitter.com/NFManagement

Bonus Material

Receive a free report on *10 Rules to Double Your Business in 90 Days*, and access to the #1 international best-selling book Lead with Livecast, at http://90days.MulticastProfits.com.

Biography

Niki Faldemolaei is the author of three #1 international best-selling books, and certified marketing technologist and strategist, Niki helps companies master the digital age so that they can grow and profit.

Niki served 20 years in corporate biotechnology and new media industries followed by 10 years in entrepreneurial product and service launches, campaigns utilizing cutting-edge intelligence and live event promotions for celebrity athletes and pioneering healers.

While working with the Newspaper Association of America, IMG Creative and Proelite, Niki achieved successful client placements in *USA Today, Newsweek, Washington Post, NY Times, Huffington Post, Muscle & Fitness*; at the Cannes Film Festival and Toronto Film Festival; as well as on the Sundance Channel, National Geographic Channel, and Showtime. Niki has also earned agency, publishing and *NY Times* interactive awards.

In her spare time she contributes to non-profit charities and was blessed to run a branch church ONAC Indigenous School of Temple Arts. Visit them at http://indigenous-nations.org.

Chapter 11: New C-Suite Stealth Tool Increases ROI

How to Exponentially Grow Revenue with Multi-Touch Attribution

by Steven Laurvick

For every executive who seeks to enhance the customer experience, generate more leads, boost sales, and increase return on investment, it is imperative that the marketing team knows which marketing campaigns and initiatives are driving revenue. Managers must be able to trust that their marketing team has legitimate data from tested and proven models before they pull the trigger on massive campaigns.

You can now implement multi-touch marketing models for your business. Technological advances make trackable, manageable, and complete revenue attribution a reality. Competent marketing teams can build models that accurately reflect each step of a consumer's trek through the entire buying cycle.

For executives in the know, this stealth technology gives them the confidence to increase their marketing budgets exponentially in order to exponentially increase ROI.

Yet currently, less than 10% of company executives will commit to a tight alignment between marketing and sales. And currently the top-performing businesses are three times as likely to measure ROI as their competitors. These current conditions allow a CEO to help his company dramatically outperform regardless of sector, market conditions or product.

A Tiny Snippet of Code Is Changing Everything

It's innocuously called a "pixel," and once inserted into the backside of your website it can dynamically change the relationship you have with your prospects and clients (and if improperly used can be a real pain in your prospects' or clients' backside).

Regardless of the consumer's choice of device, online network, or social medium, your company's marketing strategy can be transformed from a one-dimensional single-touch attribution model to multi-dimensional campaign funnels that directly target the most promising individual consumers with highly-personalized ads and messages which allow your marketing team to focus your investment on specific audiences which are most likely to buy your products and services.

The bottom line is that a remarketing pixel, if used correctly, can exponentially increase your returns on advertising spend.

Is your company retargeting?

If so, are you building multi-touch attribution models?

If you answer "no" to either question, your company is most likely destined to remain on 1st or 2nd base while your competition repeatedly hits for the cycle.

Hitting for the Cycle Loop

Home Plate = Ad is served up PPV (Pay Per View)

1st Base = Ad is clicked PPC (Pay Per Click)

2nd Base = Prospect clicks the Buy Button

3rd Base = (a) Prospect completes the purchase; or (b) Abandons the shopping cart

Home Plate = (a) Prospect clicks on an Upsell/Subscription; or (b) Is offered a down-sell

Cycle begins again.

Here's why: While virtually all marketers use multiple channels to drive sales, most still employ single-touch attribution models (usually 1st or 3rd base). Single-touch attribution models are outdated. They are limiting because they cannot track which campaigns have the biggest impact on performance, or which channels or tactics deserve credit for each conversion.

How Do Advertising Executives Perceive the Value of Attribution?

Definition of ATTRIBUTION (Webster's) "noun at·tri·bu·tion \ ą-trə-'byü-shən

1: the act of attributing; especially: the ascribing of a work (as of literature or art) to a particular author or artist

2: an ascribed quality, character, or right — at·tri·bu·tion·al \-sh(ə-)nəl\ adjective"

For marketing purposes, "attribution" is closer to the 2nd version above, an adjective that ascribes a percentage of merit or weighted value to a particular consumer action in a sales cycle.

In 2014, retargeting pioneer Adroll polled one thousand top marketing executives using their services to find out why attribution tracking matters to their company:

71% said "to understand our customers"

56% said "to understand where to apply marketing spend"

44% said "to justify marketing budget"

43% said "to optimize campaign performance"

So let's look at it from your prospect's point of view:

1.   On the way to work your prospect sees your ad on the phone...

2.   Later at work on the computer sees a search ad and clicks through to your website where they check it out...

3.   That night while on FB or Twitter or other social media on a tablet they see a retargeting ad and click on it to buy the item...

4.   Dad says "Come and eat," and the cart is abandoned...

5.   The next day at work checking Facebook (or CNN or CNBC or Pinterest, etc.) your prospect is reminded of your product and buys it.

So How Do You Attribute the Percentage of the Sale Rewarded to Which Elements of this Funnel?

Some marketing teams do one or more of the analysis below...

A.   Measure success across individual digital channels to get a better understanding of the impact that search, display ads, email, etc., have on the business.

B.   Track by device, looking at performance on mobile, television, desktop, and tablet.

C.   Businesses with brick-and-mortar in addition to online need to measure offline against online performance.

In the poll, the majority preferred the first-click/first-touch attribution model. Second went to a linear model that offered equal weight across all touchpoints in the buy cycle.

Why Should Your Team be Using a Multi-Touch Attribution Model?

Single-point attribution models lead to flawed reporting. This method discounts the impact of all other channels in the funnel; i.e., if an advertiser uses the last-touch attribution model it could lead to turning off their upper-funnel marketing campaigns because of a misplaced perception of lack of performance. This is the same way first-click models ignore the influence of subsequent ads that lead the prospect through the funnel.

Only 54% of advertisers use a multi-touch attribution model despite knowing how important and simple in concept multi-touch attribution is.

Why?

Well for starters, 80% of executives don't really trust online marketing. Another thing is that multi-touch attribution models are difficult to implement for a variety of organizational and technical reasons.

Yet it is so important and obvious that multi-touch attribution will ensure that all channels are analyzed and receive appropriate credit, give you rich insight into what drives your customers, and that the right attribution model will help you invest in the right marketing mix. In this way you are ensuring more effectively deployment of your limited resources against the highest-impact advertising programs.

Today, customers expect (and deserve) more relevant and personalized content across all channels. Executives should look at themselves as shepherds who continuously provide more innocuous ways to deliver the company brand, products and services to the consumer.

The easiest way to do that is by becoming more efficient and effective in delivering only what the prospect, buyer and client want and need. In other words most marketers are hitting their customers over the head for the sale by bombarding them with the same ads as opposed to guiding them through a well-thought-out and maintained marketing path.

Multi-Touch Models in Use Today

Here is how businesses are building effective attribution models that capture the important information, and use that data to optimize future marketing campaigns and enhance their ROI while at the same time enhancing their customer's experience.

In multi-touch campaigns, credit is given to each marketing activity that may have "touched" any completed transaction. For example, if during a six-week sales cycle, a prospect visited your brick-and-mortar store, opted into a campaign, viewed a video on your website, or watched one of your webinars, each of those marketing activities would share the revenue.

This is where subjectivity enters the playing field. Determining how much weight to give to each "touch" is always going to be relative to the condition of the field.

How does the image work in November vs. February?

Which headline converts better?

What demographic audiences create more activity?

Until testing is done, and done on an ongoing basis, you will not know which steps to weight higher or lower in terms of attribution to spend.

Attribution share will vary depending upon the business, product and/or services being offered. Some companies evenly divide credit to each touch; other companies split credit by percentages to different steps in the funnel. Factors include timing, investment, sequence, seasonality, audience, etc.

Five multi-touch attribution models:
1.   Even-split – Revenue is attributed equally for every touch.
2.   Time-decay – More weight is given for interactions that occur closer to conversion.
3.   Position-based – Greater emphasis is placed on specific touches in the cycle (usually the first and last touches).
4.   Interaction-based – More weight is placed on touches that indicate deeper engagement.
5.   Title-based – Greater emphasis is placed on touches from higher-level executives than others.

In reality these five models are a testing funnel. There will be multiple variables in each step to test and track in order to improve performance. In the beginning, to collect scientifically-sound data to test against, you would start with even attribution across all steps and change the weightings on subsequent campaigns using the more sophisticated models below it.

Experts such as Adroll, Adwords and Perfect Audience recommend long enough time frames for campaigns to run in order to not over- or under-value the impact of each step. After you have enough data to analyze revenue results, a duplicate campaign with different weightings (variable ad spends) can be deployed based on the results.·

Finally, remember that you should be shepherding your prospect, buyer, client through your sales funnel by using expirations in your retargeting campaigns. In other words, the tracking pixel should not target the buyer with the same ad used when she was a prospect; and the client should not be targeted with the same ad as when she was a buyer; and expiration dates allow your campaigns to both be more consumer-friendly AND decrease retargeted marketing costs.

Final Analysis
I believe the reason most companies have still not implemented multi-touch attribution marketing campaigns is that it is difficult

to find the end result desired from which to build forward. Because it is so cutting-edge, retargeted marketing requires a leap of faith by executives to trust their team with unproven models, and most marketing managers do not have a handle on the funnel they have to build, nor how to set up the testing they will have to conduct to sell it to the front office.

Should the budget to drive online interaction be spent on Facebook, Twitter and other social media? If so, what allocation should go to each medium?

Should the budget for search be left alone, decreased, or increased if social media retargeting is initiated? Should the budget for email and SMS text be raised or lowered?

Can we use search and our client list in tandem with the new retargeting campaign?

How do we track all of this and determine weighting for each touch point?

I know that if you deploy the correct systems using the right tools, these questions can be answered with more confidence than ever.

As of the time of the writing of this chapter (November 2015) more than half of all U.S. business-to-business marketing companies have no multi-touch attribution models set up for their own company. If most marketing companies are still in the dark, imagine how many companies in your industry have no clue about this new "stealth" technology.

If your company sets up a model that tracks every client action in the buying cycle, from the batter's box to home plate, you will learn what drives your prospects and know what and how to sell to them over and over again. Early implementation and persistent testing will position your company to trounce the competition and build revenue on a consistent basis.

Contact Steven Laurvick
www.channelmarketingagency.com
www.enablemobility.com
www.thesandiegobusinessdirectory.com

steve@askame.com
steve@how-to-increase-sales.com

Linkedin.com/SteveLaurvick
Facebook.com/StevenLaurvick
Twitter.com/slaurvick

Bonus Material

To get the *Channel Marketing Agency Multi-Touch Workbook*, text your name and email to: steve@csuite.channelmarketingagency. com. Or go to: http://www.Csuite.ChannelMarketingAgency.com and begin implementing your attribution model right now. Go get the worksheet, give it to your marketing manager, and get them to implement one or more of these models today. Make no mistake – measuring revenue will make for a more successful marketing team.

Biography

Steven Laurvick is a best-selling author, business owner and marketing consultant. His marketing company has published eight titles in paperback, e-book and audio formats. His first best seller, *Oracular Marketing: How to Build an Evergreen Online Marketing Platform*

for Your Business, Products and Services, is a marketing manual for small business start-ups.

As the moderator of the podcasts *The Online Marketing Guy and Caregiver Support,* Steve has interviewed dozens of thought leaders, medical device inventors, manufacturers and business owners. His international #1 best seller, *How the Experts Make More Money in Less Time: In-Depth Interviews with 9 Cross-Channel Marketing Professionals,* is a compilation of the transcripts of the best interviews conducted by Steve on *The Online Marketing Guy* video podcast.

The owner of EnableMobility.com, MedAme.com, WheelchairShowers.com and other online venues with over 3,000 medical products, he is an expert at marketing on Amazon, Facebook, Pinterest, Twitter, Instagram, eBay, Shopify, WooCommerce, Google Merchant and other venues for physical and digital products online.

A certified consultant with over 100 Instant Customer/TPNI Engage client sessions, Steve has helped dozens of entrepreneurs and business owners achieve success by consulting on the use of CRM systems with video marketing, email and SMS text messaging, and setting up automated social media delivery systems.

His company AME LLC is a marketing company that uses retargeted marketing, app creation, video production, webcast production, SEO, affiliate marketing, and PPC promotions.

Chapter 12: Killer Keywords that Kick

Attract and Keep the RIGHT Customers...How keywords can revolutionize how you communicate with your customers

by Jerry Dreessen

OK - OK - OK....

I get it. Keyword research is considered a technical job, and for some ... boring. Got it. So why read a whole chapter on it? Simple: companies should never leave their business in the hands of someone who can control their search engine placement and their future marketing with online customer search traffic.

And now that I have your attention....

When businesses place their service or product online, they assume/hope people will find them. They have spent 12-15% of their budget in marketing and are looking for a great return on their investment. Aren't we all?

The amount of online searches has increased significantly in the last five years. Six in 10 adults have done research online about the products and services BEFORE they buy (68%), up from 49% in 2004 (1). A more recent compilation of data states that number has climbed even higher:

"81% of shoppers conduct online research before they make a purchase. 60% begin by using a search engine to find the products they want, and 61% will read product reviews before making any purchase. On average, a consumer will visit three stores before making their purchase." (2)

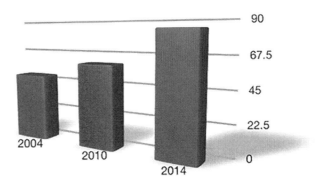

online searches

What that boils down to is this. Having the correct keywords in any/all online articles and web pages is essential to attracting the types of clients and buyers businesses are looking for. Not using the techniques SEO companies like mine teach can leave businesses buried deep in the search engines, never seeing the light of day, nor generating leads and sales, or even worse – being #2 to a rival company.

Currently there are two types of internet users – those who want to *learn* about something and those who want to *buy* something. Having a clear, focused image of "who" a business is selling to will make a huge difference in time and money spent on marketing.

Most companies have already spent time and money designing that "who" into their "avatar." The avatar then helps set and design the demographics (where they are) as well as the psychographics (how and where they like to buy) to attract their ultimate client. Let's start first by focusing on the main avatar type, the buyer.

The Buyer (or Referrer)

The buyers have a rough idea of what they want, or know exactly what they want, and now they are trying to find the best price, which also includes shipping and handling. Most of their time (usually 30 minutes to an hour) is spent typing in various search phrases for the exact product they want to buy.

They are inundated with search engine ads above and to the right of their computer screen. Sometimes what is shown in those little ads is exactly what they are searching for, which leads to another click, but not always the exact product they want.

Proper keyword placement for companies spending money on Pay-Per-Click (PPC) ads can reap major rewards if they have a great keyword strategy. PPC campaigns are often created by the very same marketing company that businesses are paying money to for the placement of the ads. It's like putting the fox in charge of the hen house.

The less businesses know about PPC, they less they will realize how much money can be wasted on PPC ad campaigns that are getting clicked on by "window shoppers" or those just seeking information, or lead a buyer to a page that doesn't have what they are looking for on it.

A company that strategizes and picks only the keywords buyers are looking for, and sends them to the exact product the ad talks about, can maximize profits and reduce their PPC campaign budget, increase their ROI and make CEOs happy. There are many courses that teach how to achieve PPC success, and there are many businesses that provide theses great services. It all boils down to how to price out a budget; or as I like to say: Price, Time and Quality – pick two of them.

For the buyer that is shopping online, it's their *experience once they are on the businesses/product website* that makes them want to follow through to the most exciting part, *the final sale.*

Looking at the website's font type and size, the colors of the background, header, border lines, the quality of the photos, the audio and HD quality of the videos – all of these help create the setting or mood, as if it were the entrance into a shop or boutique. In fact, to make a buyer's search time easier, successful businesses are also including keywords that their buyers use, making a connection with articles via hyperlinks, links to in-site pages, FAQs, 20-30-second explanation regarding HD quality videos, etc.

Lauren Kaye, at Brafton Inc., writes "Digital content IS becoming a deal breaker for consumers (especially younger buyers) who are looking for information online. Companies that aren't there with answers to prospects' questions will fall off the radar, while brands that anticipate questions and provide useful resources will win brand awareness and, eventually, conversions."

The companies with websites that anticipate the needs of the shoppers, and can provide instant answers, will have much higher conversions and sales. Keeping the pulse of the top social media websites, and if any new slang terms are getting created that they can quickly take advantage of, will be able to update the content of their websites, create new content, and keep the SEO algorithms happy, as well as watch their web pages rise to the top of the search engines and increase traffic and sales.

On the other hand, businesses that have a site that does not allow the buyer a chance to see the product, or learn more about it, such as the entire cost of shipping and handling, will begin to see a lot of abandoned shopping carts. The keen companies that do market research plus allow a shopper to go online and critique their sites will gain amazing insight into design and ease of use for the consumer.

It is important to recognize how essential it is to stay ahead of, or on top, of the trending curve. Imagine a person searching with a new buzzword on the Internet and just happens to find a business that sells a product or service that either IS that buzzword, or is a product/ service that makes that trendy buzzword object appear even more sparkly and shiny.

The new product would get instant viral social network sharing and ride the wave of that buzz as if it were initially part of the trend as well. Not only will buyers appreciate knowing the businesses they are shopping with know their culture, but the other type of Internet user mentioned above, the learner, will also appreciate it too.

The Learner

The learner is actually two different types. One subtype is doing research for a project, or just personal edification; and the other subtype is a POTENTIAL buyer. Businesses need to realize that learners are also buyers – *they just don't know it yet.* Creating informative articles and videos that teach, and include using their products or services in those videos using key buzzwords or trending keywords or possibly giving away FREE SAMPLES, will plant a seed deep into the corpus callosum of the learner.

The *learner* will continue to research the trend or keyword, maybe even share their knowledge online with their friends or through social media, and when the time comes, when they are ready to buy, or if a friend of theirs is looking for that particular product, they will recall that company and complete the intended journey outcome designed by the marketing department and become a *buyer* or a *referrer*.

The companies that recognize the power and potential of keywords, and how they will affect their business and online (desktop and mobile) sales will have the most growth going into 2020. Creating a great mobile app can also play a part in the decision making of online buyers, who use their mobile devices more and more to do research and make purchases. Companies that offer a free app, and can create great engagement with clients are also apt to make more sales.

Companies like Pivotal, based in Santa Monica, Seattle and New York, are seeing a significant rise in businesses seeking out new and innovative apps for mobile users. The businesses that want to be the lead dog against their competition would be wise to look into mobile apps, and offer a free download on their main website (which should also be mobile-friendly).

So, how does a business continue forward into the 2020s, generate more business and increase their online traffic? Keywords.

Keywords that help a buyer: (1) find, (2) learn and (3) trust the company they are about to exchange cash for a product or a service with. A company that can *speak their language*, knows their "slang" and terminology. As I mentioned above, it is important to stay on top of the trend. Learning about a new way to use a product or service, or

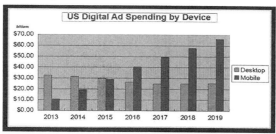

discovering a new word, or viral video that ties into a company's style can be turned into a ton of traffic to their eStore or business site if it is handled correctly.

Google, Bing and Yahoo! all have the same goal, and that is to bring new, relevant content to the searcher (and to monetize it). That is what makes their visitors come back for more. These search engines all have their own special artificial intelligence robots or "spiders" which crawl the web in search of new content, and then update their databases to provide that new information to their users.

Websites that are easy to read or are "spider friendly," and contain content that is congruent with the main keywords for the website or business, called LSI (Latent Semantic Indexing) will gain favor with the search engine databases. The combination of new or fresh content and its relevancy will always outrank stagnant websites that are no longer relevant.

Businesses that identify core keywords for their business can begin to "diversify their keyword portfolio" and create new content, which in turn becomes updated website material, and stimulates the spiders to update and reindex their website.

Successful keyword research for businesses of all shapes and sizes begins with a core keyword set. It usually starts with a [product] + [avatar] + [ingredients]. Brainstorming and whiteboards are very common in "keyword war rooms" within a successful business.

Companies that are moving forward in today's online world are also working with keyword research companies that help them drill down to keyword phrases using core "selling" or "buying" components. However, just because a company has a great group of keywords, and they place them on their website, doesn't mean they will be on the first page of the main search engines.

Companies that rely on great core keywords and LSI keywords also recognize this final website marketing component: Keyword Competition (KWC). KWC can be the death of a company if it isn't aware of the competition and what it takes to outrank all the other websites offering the same product or service. Keyword research companies are often divided into many branches; keyword creation or research, keyword LSI, website keyword optimization, PPC keywords, and keyword competition, to name a few.

Keywords also have their own ranking and price. For example, a company can rank #1 for a top keyword IF they are willing to spend top dollar for the #1 PPC position. When a buyer/referrer/learner clicks on that ad, the company is charged for the click (hence PAY per click). These keywords can cost as little as .001 or up to and more than $500 each time they get clicked on.

The reason the price can get so high is because a keyword cost is based on the amount each competitor is willing to pay for that keyword to display their ad on the top of page one in the search engines. This can be very expensive, unless a company knows exactly what they are doing, and can convert more "clickers" into buyers than just "clickers." PPC campaigns on average rarely contain such high-priced keywords, which can make using PPC cost-effective.

A group of businesses that sell the same product, and have done their research realize that the most searches done each day by buyers for their product enter in the search engine "search bar" 5 to 10 common keyword phrases. These businesses know that their "avatars" only use those phrases to find them online. The businesses then take their ads, place a "top bid" or an amount that they are willing to pay to have their PPC ad clicked on to send the customer to their website or product page. If their bid is the highest of all the competition, they will have the top placement, or #1 position in the top right corner of that search engine on page one.

A good keyword strategist will also know how to find keywords that have high traffic (or searches) and the lowest PPC bid. For example, let's say keyword #1 is a very highly-competitive word and has a PPC cost of $25.20, and has around 3,000 searches a day. Keyword #2 has only 1,800 searches a day, and costs $7.00 a click. Keyword #3 is $3.21 a click and has 1300 searches a day.

The KW strategist could create an ad campaign that is shown to around 3,000 searches/people a day, at $25.20/click, OR the same ad in front of 3,100 people/searches a day averaging a cost of $5.10 a click. If Keywords #2 and #3 have less competition than keyword #1 (usually the case), the company they are working for should get more traffic, more clicks, and a larger ROI for their marketing dollar.

Organic Keywords vs. PPC

Another way for websites to get traffic and NOT have to pay PPC costs to get traffic is through the keyword optimization of their website. The spiders crawl the website, organizing words on the website, and create a keyword database list for the site. Here is where an expert SEO/SEM/Keyword strategist can do the most good, while a person who "thinks they know how to do it" could potentially send their company's website into the digital abyss.

This is the realm known as "organic" search engine results. When a buyer or learner queries a search in their favorite search engine, the database collected by the spiders pulls up the all the web pages that show those keywords in various places on its site, and puts them in order from #1 to hundreds of thousands.

The web page or website or video or article or review site that has the best ranking goes in the #1 organic spot on the page (the first one just below any paid ads). The second best-optimized/relevant page/video/article/review goes in the #2 spot, and so on, until the top 10 spots have filled up page one.

These organic spots do not cost any money to be there, or to be clicked on. These are the prime spots companies pay large amounts of money to occupy as well, based on the competitiveness of the keyword, and the amount of daily traffic a #1 spot brings. Local, small companies, without any competition, on the other hand, only have to put up a single-page website with proper keyword optimization to dominate page one for the city they do business in.

Since there are no costs to pay to be clicked on, businesses often try all kinds of tactics to stay at the #1 spot. Doing it the right way will keep their spot for a very long time (close to eternity). Doing it the wrong way will cause their site to get "slapped" or "sandboxed," and knocked out of the first 10 pages or first 100 spots until they can remove these "black-hat" techniques. Oftentimes SEO groups will learn of new "back door" methods that the spider bots don't know about, and begin implementing these tactics for fast placement. If it is deemed "unfair" by the search engine companies, they will update their indexing.

Once the search engines announce their new indexing algorithms, all heck breaks loose as major companies scramble to make sure their SEO/SEM/LSI tactics are compliant, or face a severe slapping.

Any company that has a competitive online presence soon realizes the importance of keywords, and how they can make or break their online awareness to buyers. Some companies don't worry at all about organic listings, and spend their marketing money on PPC, which sends buyers to their website, where a sales conversion is made.

Others spend their marketing dollars building up an organic presence and share in the 85% click rate the top three spots on page one get, without having to spend money on PPC campaigns.

And of course there are the companies that spend money and time doing both. It all depends on how much the final product costs, and the costs to bring a buyer to the site, and of those that are on the site, convert to be a buyer.

Keyword strategists can help companies look at their marketing costs and estimate what it can cost per paying customer, and determine which marketing strategy will work the best for them.

Keeping an Open Mind for New Keywords

Some companies and their owners can become locked into who they are, what they sell, and never wander outside of that online marketing "box." The avatar they created hasn't changed in years. Understanding keywords, trends, and "symbiotic" keywords can open the doors to new types of buyers and traffic that was never thought to exist when they first opened their doors (or "eDoors") for business.

For example, let's pretend there is a company that specializes in dark chocolate. They spend their marketing budget on people who love chocolate. They sell dark chocolate to lots of people. They have a great website, lots of great pictures, images, videos, reviews, press releases, and an easy-to-use shopping cart system, as well as a mobile app. Sounds like a great story with a happy ending, right?

But what if they could expand their sales (using the same products) by doing keyword research and come up with other "avatars" or buyers who are already searching for AND WANTING TO BUY their product? These would be people who are doing research and learning about different types of dark chocolate or dark chocolate main ingredients, for example.

They may have an affinity to the different percentages of dark chocolate, or want to belong to the "78% Dark Chocolate Club," or the "Dark Chocolate of the Month Club." A Facebook page created by the company, which updates 2-3 times a day with interesting content, and special offers on their chocolate could begin to increase traffic.

There may be people who are searching as well for "Theobroma cacao seeds" for studies on health benefits, or antioxidants. They may be doing a research paper just on "antioxidants." Creating web pages that address the learner crowd that is surfing for information, and finding our dark chocolate company's web page on "The Benefits of Dark Chocolate: Antioxidants and the Theobroma cacao seed," the learner may find a page that is chock-full of images, research, videos – all the information a learner would need to do a research paper on, or a quote for their research paper, or a new link to tell their friends or teacher about.

The other great thing about it is they may want to order a bar or two as they begin to like and trust this dark chocolate company. The "share this with your friends" button on the site makes it even easier for them to tell their friends about the company – or if they are a blogger and are doing a review, there may have been a section on the site titled: "Doing a review of the benefits of dark chocolate? Enter your name and address and e-mail address and we'll ship out a FREE sample to you!"

Now they have captured a learner's name, email and address, given them "above and beyond" what they were looking for, and possibly turned them into a raving fan as they feature the company on their "All About Chocolate" blog with a fan base of over 100K. Even though that makes for a happy ending, and allowed the company a chance to "think outside the box," and creating thousands in sales for a huge ROI, the story doesn't have to end here.

In fact, that's just the surface of what keywords can do for a company. Would you believe me if I told you there are still more keywords, traffic and customers that can be attracted to this company? In fact, I'm about to demonstrate a keyword search that will show traffic for this company in a way they may never have thought of, and that it can earn possibly 10-15% more business to their overall bottom line – from a group of clients that are desperately searching for them, and neither one knowing the other exists!

When a company begins to do keyword research on things other than the obvious like "chocolate lovers" and "dark chocolate lovers" they are able to expand into new markets. As I mentioned at the beginning of this chapter, there is a *third component* to the core keyword set – *ingredients*. And in this case, "dark chocolate ingredients" will take this company's keyword research to a new group of people: *smokers.*

People who are trying to quit smoking, to be exact.

According to The Society of Thoracic Surgeons, *about 1.1 billion people on our planet smoke (4). Recent statistics list a whopping 70% want to quit altogether* (5). What a huge market! Seventy percent of ONE BILLION. That's a LOT of people who are trying to quit smoking, if I've done my math correctly (and without a spreadsheet).

During my keyword research of dark chocolate and the main ingredients, I found research articles that talked about dark chocolate and how it helps people quit smoking. The articles talk about the specific ingredients in dark chocolate, and how it helps soothe the cravings.

What a great niche to expand into if you are a dark chocolate company. All that company needs to do is write some articles, press releases, create some videos, and link them to their website, feature a page or a menu header specifically for smokers who want to quit, and monitor the traffic that comes to their website as a result.

And what about all the apps that are out there to help people quit smoking? Why not create a quit-smoking app that sells dark chocolate? The smokers that are looking for ways to quit will be searching online to learn about the natural ways to quit, and the natural ingredients they can buy to help them out. The dark chocolate company that seizes this opportunity and provides all the research to turn a learner into a buyer will carpe diem.

Anyone know a smoker that doesn't have friends that smoke? And how many of them want to quit? And how many of them would love to get a FREE sample of dark chocolate by entering their name, email, and address (and the company can begin their lead capture autoresponder campaign)? And what company that sells dark chocolate wouldn't want to improve their bottom line and help people become more healthy?

All of this from keyword research. Pretty cool, huh?

As businesses make the plunge into the Internet, define their niche, their avatar, their product, and ingredients or components, more and more different kinds of keywords begin to make more sense. Companies that specialize in keyword research have all the latest technology and tracking information to give more "bang for the buck" to generate more traffic for the companies that hire them to help search and expand their market share.

Companies that have a basic understanding of what makes a "good" keyword vs. a "bad" keyword, or a "cheap/expensive PPC campaign" no longer have to panic or feel like they are being held hostage to keyword research companies that may be preying on their ignorance. Businesses with this knowledge can finally start seeing real value in the extensive research, and have an understanding about the need to make changes for a better buyer/learner experience. And that will generate more traffic and more sales.

Now *that* is a happy ending, indeed.

Notes

(1)   http://www.pewinternet.org/2010/09/29/online-product-research

(2)   http://www.adweek.com/socialtimes/81-shoppers-conduct-online-research-making-purchase-infographic/208527

(3)   http://www.brafton.com/news/94-percent-b2b-buyers-research-online-purchase-decisions

(4)   https://www.sharecare.com/health/quit-smoking/how-many-world-smoke-cigarettes

(5)   http://www.statisticbrain.com/quitting-smoking-statistics

Contact Jerry Dreessen
whoisyourwebguy@gmail.com
www.whoisyourwebguy.com

Bonus Material
Watch "over my shoulder" as I do keyword research for the fictitious "Dark Chocolate Company" can click on or enter this link in their browser: http://www.whoisyourwebguy.com/CSuiteOTS.

FREE 30-minute keyword research session. Let me help you find 5-10 high-volume, low-competition keywords, or the top 100 keywords your top three competitors are using. http://www.whoisyourwebguy.com/30minKWSession

Biography

Jerry Dreessen has been studying and implementing keyword search and website optimization since 2008. He is constantly learning the latest techniques and is always testing new and creative ways to bring clients' content to the "front of the search engine line" to generate organic as well as paid traffic. He holds a Certification in

Author Expert Marketing Machines, as well as being CEO of Who Is Your Webguy, a local and national client-marketing company.

He is a master close-up magician, with three original illusions on the market; and in his spare time sails Hobie Cats with his wife, Jenny. He is happily married with three kids, and is not so happily an owner of three cats.

Chapter 13: Building Profitable Customer Relationships

The Three Key Marketing and Sales Communication Frameworks that Growing Businesses Have in Common

by Ian Bosler

Before diving right in to the three marketing and sales frameworks, I need to challenge your thinking about how your business organizes its marketing and sales communications activities.

The three key frameworks need to operate within an environment that is designed to facilitate the communication processes. Otherwise their effectiveness will be limited.

Finding Your Optimum Marketing and Sales Process

Ask yourself this simple question: Do you operate with an optimal marketing and sales process?

The chances are the honest answer is no. In fact from my experience, over 90% of businesses don't even recognize that marketing and sales activities should be designed and operated as an end-to-end and integrated process let alone an optimized process.

Right now you might be picturing the traditional marketing and sales funnel; and in so doing you're making a grave mistake in thinking that is a good process model. Throwing a handful of prospects into the top of the funnel and hoping a few will convert to a sale is not a process.

Instead, think of how Henry Ford managed to revolutionize the motor vehicle industry by dramatically reducing the time and cost required to build his Model T Ford.

While I wasn't around when he devised the Model T Ford, I can guarantee that he didn't see his production process as a funnel where you throw in nuts, bolts, engines, body parts, etc., and miraculously (with the help of gravity) a completed Model T Ford just "popped out." So why design marketing and sales processes using such flawed logic?

Symptoms That Your Process Is Broken

1.   The finger of blame. This is the most common symptom where you will hear Sales blaming Marketing that the leads are too few or of poor quality, while Marketing blames Sales for poor follow-up or not understanding what they are trying to sell,

2.   Employee dissatisfaction and churn. This may be the result of the "finger of blame game" but more often it's born from frustration as members of the marketing and sales teams know that they can perform better but are hamstrung by an inability to influence upstream and downstream activities,

3.   Inconsistent brand story across marketing and sales activities. This isn't as obvious; but a quick comparison of marketing materials and sales proposals will often reveal a disconnect.

4.   Increased cost of marketing and sales. The cost of marketing and sales as a percentage of revenue is a key metric most growing companies measure. (You do this, don't you?) An optimal marketing and sales process will continually deliver a lower cost ratio over time.

Benefits

1. Accountability

We have all heard the saying: "Half of my advertising is wasted; trouble is I don't know which half." Well I'm here to tell you that this is rubbish. This kind of brainwashing has been around since marketing and sales were invented and are designed to avoid accountability. Over 30 years ago, my mentor at the time pointed out that this premise was a lie; and I have since discovered that by creating a true marketing and sales process you can quickly and easily generate metrics across all activities that leave nobody a place to hide.

2. Lower Cost and Higher Productivity

A well-designed process has clearly-defined inputs, activities, and outputs. It becomes very easy to apply lean manufacturing principles to the process to reduce wasted activities, and in so doing reduce time.

3. Automation: Supercharge Your Productivity Gains

Who doesn't want to supercharge their results? Today's marketing and sales automation tools are so low-cost and have such a massive ROI that you would have to be crazy not to be using them. However, be careful that you're not supercharging a flawed process. Otherwise they can have the opposite effect.

4. Consistent Branding That Will Add Extra Horsepower to Your Efforts

Inconsistent branding is the bane of all professional marketers. It's costly to establish a brand, but even more costly to continually manage, monitor, and correct deviations from your brand story. A clearly-defined process that identifies all the customer touch-points makes the job of your "brand police" much easier.

5. Scalable

It's not much use if your process can't be scaled. By following these approaches you will greatly increase the probability of business growth. However, trust me; you don't want to have to rebuild your processes every time your business has a growth spurt, so build in scalability from the start.

Three Core Frameworks

I'm regularly asked the secret to my many business successes. Often, before I've had a chance to respond, it's quickly followed with: "Do you use ... (add the latest bright and shiny marketing object)?"

Forget the latest Bright and Shiny Object (BSO). They simply won't work unless you have the basics in place. When it comes to building profitable customer relationships there are only three basic marketing and sales communication activities that you need to worry about. It's only when you get these in place will the latest BSOs have any hope of delivering results.

Put simply, the following three communication frameworks are all you need to set your business up for success:

1. Attract New Customers
2. Sell More to Existing Customers
3. Charge Higher Prices

I know, it sounds logical and should be simple to do. However, I believe the vast number of Marketing & Sales BSOs that hit the market are distracting businesses from getting the basics in place.

Attract New Customers

Attract the right ones by giving value up front to prospects who match your criteria for the ideal client. Sounds logical and simple; however most businesses screw this up.

Avoid the temptation to shout at your prospects; it doesn't work. You probably don't appreciate sales messages being rammed down your throat; and I think I'm right that your prospects and clients don't like it either. Then why do so many businesses persist with this outdated and unproductive approach?

We all like to work with great clients; so start with defining your ideal client and have all your marketing and sales materials tuned to talk to that person. For most, the ideal client profile is usually sitting under their noses. Look to your client database (You have one don't you?), as the answer lies in there. The key is to recognize them. Don't be tempted to gravitate immediately to the client you have a great personal relationship with. Rather, you should look for key behaviors that match your business values and characteristics that will support your growth objectives.

Speaking to your ideal client will help you avoid the trap of trying to communicate to everyone, the result of which is that you will communicate to no one. This is a difficult thing for most people to do, as it can be counterintuitive. When you communicate to your ideal client profile, you will attract and engage with others, which is okay. However you need to have a good selection process to weed out those clients that won't support your objectives.

Your framework needs to "qualify out" prospects. Again this may seem counterintuitive especially for salespeople who are rewarded based on revenue. Watch your reward system. It must match the behavior and objectives you want to achieve. Otherwise you will "get what you pay for."

Provide value with content that will enrich your ideal client's life. If you're selling to businesses, your content should be tuned to enhancing their business life, while if you're consumer-orientated it needs to enhance their personal life. This approach positions your business as the expert in your field and will attract and educate ideal prospects until they are ready to buy. But this is only part of the story.

Your process needs to engage with these prospects as they go through their buying process. Good engagement-processes also facilitates your prospect sharing your content to their networks, gaining a low-cost but massive boost to your marketing efforts. A fully-engaged prospect will make the sales effort required to convert them to a customer simple, easy and fast.

When was the last time you asked your customers to help promote your business? The easiest way to do this is to ask for a testimonial or a case study, and the best time to ask is right after they have bought something. A good marketing and sales communications process will have this simple request automatically deployed at the right time; and the output becomes marketing content ready-made for distribution.

Finally, don't forget to seek direct referrals from existing customers. A good referral facilitates the transfer of trust to potential customers, shortening the sales cycle and often results in larger deals. But don't forget to define a good referral for your customers; and providing some communication tools will make their lives easier.

Sell More to Existing Customers

We have all heard the saying: "It costs 10 times less to sell to an existing customer than it does to find a new one." This concept is often lost in the day-to-day battle to win customers. However, if it's built into your marketing and sales process it will happen on autopilot.

Up-Selling: There are always people who prefer to buy the more expensive option. This may be because of the additional features in the offer, or they may have the perception that the higher-priced package will better solve their problems. Whatever the motivation, providing an upgrade path will lead to higher average-order value and usually higher margins.

Cross-Selling: McDonald's is a master at this: "Would you like fries with your order?" It's such a simple thing to do; but failure to build it into your process means that you will leave "money on the table" while reducing the overall customer experience.

Expand the Offer: Expanding the offer will outperform cross- and up-selling every day of the week. This approach forms the basis of the Blue Ocean Strategy, which not only expands the value of a sale, it also shifts the landscape to render your competition irrelevant.

To achieve this, you need to understand your customer's value chain and where your products and services fit within it. When you expand your offer up and down the value chain, it suddenly becomes easier to communicate holistic time and cost savings while increasing your average order size and margins ... besides customers love it as it usually makes their business model simpler and more efficient.

Repeat Sales: There is nothing sweeter than a returning customer. They already know, like, and trust you so the follow-up sales effort should be easy. Why then do most businesses suffer from what is known as "follow-up failure"? It seems that a lot of focus is placed on attracting and converting prospects, which often results in the neglect of a very lucrative revenue stream.

This isn't hard to fix especially with an automated marketing and sales process. The system can take care of the communicating as long as the platform has been populated with the appropriate content, and the database triggers have been set up correctly.

Charge Higher Prices

Business nirvana is selling more and at higher prices. Achieve this then all your other business problems become mere annoyances.

The Prize Goes to the Expert: Remember the old saying: "Nobody ever gets fired for hiring IBM." The fact is people are prepared to pay higher prices to whom they perceive to be the industry leader as they believe they will be better able to fix the problem they are trying to solve. The key takeaway here is to ensure that all your marketing and sales communications are tuned to position you as the industry leader, while avoiding some of the price communications traps that drive customers mad or force them to compare you to others on price.

Don't Bury Prices: Do you avoid having the price discussion? This is a trap so many businesses fall into. They either avoid the discussion altogether or bury the price in the detail of their proposals. This drives customers mad as they need a price base to make informed decisions. What works best is to reveal the price up front and then turn the discussion to the benefits the customer will receive from making the investment. The customer will, in their mind, look for how your proposal justifies the price; job done.

Don't Force Price Comparisons: Do you force your customers and prospects to make supplier comparisons based on price? The printing industry is one of the worst offenders of this dumb mistake, but the disease has spread to many other industries.

I don't get why so many businesses rely on their Management Information System (MIS) to automatically generate quotes. They, in effect, have delegated one of the most important sales communication tools to unknown software engineers and accountants. No wonder they force their customers to make price-based choices. If this is happening in your business, you need to stop it immediately.

Only Provide Proposals: By eliminating quotations from your business, your Marketing & Sales team will need to develop powerful and high-converting proposals. Do this right and your average sales value will skyrocket along with margins and you will experience an appreciable reduction in the sales cycle.

Get this right and you will also enjoy:

• Brand consistency right through to sales conversion and beyond. It doesn't add one cent to your costs to produce all your communications in a coordinated and "on brand" manner. Chances are your competitors don't do this, which makes it easy to stand out and get noticed for all the right reasons.

•   Communicating your Unique Value Proposition (UVP), which will not only strengthen your proposal but will make it easier for your customers to identify the value you deliver and thus justify your pricing.

•   By including additional items in your product bundle, you will differentiate your offer and move the competitor comparison away from a simple price compare.

•   Including testimonials and case studies will encourage new customers to provide additional marketing material. After all, who doesn't want to see their name up in lights?

•   Speed up the sales cycle by removing or limiting the purchasing risk. Fully communicate your guarantee and don't just rely on a symbol or guarantee logo. You probably don't have to offer any more than the industry norm or legislated customer protections. Just the fact that you communicate them properly will make you stand apart from most of your competitors.

Case Study: The Intertype Story

The author knows this business very well. It is one of his ventures, a printing business, which he founded in 2004.

In 2008 the business was deeply impacted by the Global Financial Crisis, the effect of which was compounded with the emergence of a significant shift in the landscape of the printing industry. This necessitated a dramatic re-think of how the business operated, and in particular how the marketing and sales activities where organized. Back then the business followed the industry norm of limited marketing activities but heavy investment in expensive sales resources. This had to change because it no longer worked and it was drowning under the costs.

Prior to the changes, Intertype's results mirrored the printing industry. The following table shows the movement in some key areas.

	Then	Now
Revenue Growth	-4%	13%
Net Margin	7%	22%
Number in Sales Team	4	0.5
Cost of Marketing & Sales (% of revenue)	18%	7%
Average Order Size	$564	$1,986
Average Days Outstanding	58	7

So what changed?

Understanding What Customer Problems Intertype Solved

The printing industry was suffering with reduced demand and commoditized pricing, so the decision was made to stop looking to the industry for answers. The business needed new thinking and new ways to engage with prospects and customers while leveraging existing core capabilities.

When looked at from a customer's perspective, printing is just another medium to aid communication. Digging deeper into the problems that Intertype's customers were trying to solve revealed that they were really looking to improve the results and speed of their marketing and sales communications. It is interesting to note that this also was the problem Intertype needed to solve for its own survival.

Creating a Process

The existing marketing and sales process, while consistent with the printing industry, was clearly not working. New thinking and approaches were needed which required extensive research and investment in training with organizations outside of the industry.

Key requisites included ensuring the processes could be automated and quickly deployed, while being easy for users to operate. At the time, there were a limited number of automation tools available. However, the functionality and interconnectivity continues to evolve which opens up exciting new opportunities every year.

Focused on the Three Core Frameworks

The three core frameworks were foundational requirements of the redesigned marketing and sales process. This simplified the performance measurement and refining processes which resulted in the rapid turnaround of the business. In fact, results became evident in only six weeks.

Business Redefined

By 2010, Intertype was longer recognized as a printing business. Rather, it had evolved to become a marketing and sales communications business. Since the change, the business continued on a stellar growth trajectory with performance far out-stripping the industry it has left behind.

Contact Ian Bosler

ian@intertype.com.au
http://www.intertype.com.au
http://www.informationproductmastery.com
https://au.linkedin.com/in/ianbosler

Bonus Material

Visit http://www.threeframeworks.com to access free in-depth video training on how you can establish the three essential marketing and sales communication frameworks in your business.

Biography

Ian Bosler has published three International #1 Bestselling business books and is a serial entrepreneur. After a very successful corporate career in senior marketing and sales roles, he founded Intertype in 2004. Intertype started as a typical printing business but is now helping small, medium and large businesses to unlock profitable growth by improving their marketing and sales communications.

He has been involved with the printing industry for over 30 years. From large multinational companies to his own start-up, Ian's printing experience encompasses packaging, business forms, commercial print, mail house, security printing, digital printing, and print management.

During his time at these organizations he worked closely with senior executives of major corporations in Australia, UK, USA, and throughout Asia. This exposed him to the communication processes across most industry sectors including Banking & Finance, Education, Manufacturing, Mining, Insurance, as well as all levels of government.

While there have been many achievements throughout his career, his biggest success has come from his own start-up printing company which he founded in 2004. This business has evolved to provide comprehensive marketing and sales communications products and services to an enviable list of Australian and international clients.

By deploying a highly-automated marketing and sales communications approach within his own printing business, it has been recognized by the printing industry heavyweight, Fuji Xerox, as representing the model for the future of the printing industry.

Originally from Mudgee, a small country town in Australia, he now lives with his wife and son in Melbourne. He loves the ocean, is a keen sailor, and enjoys indoor archery.

Bonus Materials

Buyers of the Build to Grow book gain access to a range of free bonuses including:

Additional books and workbooks,

Video training and assessment tools,

Strategy sessions, and much more

Simply visit www.buildtogrowbook.com or scan the QR code to gain easy access to all the free bonuses.

Michael Alf

Download the PDF version of my #1 best-selling book *The Virtual Summit Formula,* which describes the 7 stage virtual summit process at http://tiny.cc/csuite.

And when you have questions or want to discuss your virtual summit please get in touch at michael@virtualsummitformula.com.

I can also be reached on LinkedIn at https://www.linkedin.com/in/michaelalfmel

Ian Bosler

Visit http://www.threeframeworks.com to access free in-depth video training on how you can establish the three essential marketing and sales communication frameworks in your business.

Ian can be reached at ian@intertype.com.au and on LinkedIn at https://au.linkedin.com/in/ianbosler. You can also visit his main business sites at http://www.intertype.com.au or www.informationproductmastery.com.

Karol Clark

Verify the health of your organization and gain access to free customizable healthy employee tools at www.HealthyCorpQuiz.com. You can also reach Karol Clark at Karol@CFWLS.com, on LinkedIn at https://www.linkedin.com/in/clarkkarol, and visit her business sites at:

www.CFWLS.com, www.WeightLossPracticeBuilder.com, and www.YourBestSellerBook.com.

Jerry Dreessen

Get your FREE 30-Minute keyword research session. Let me help you find 5-10 high volume, low competition keywords, or the top 100 keywords your top 3 competitors are using. Visit: http://www.whoisyourwebguy.com/30minKWSession.

Miguel de Jesús

Get my free eBook *Let Your Emotional Intelligence Do the Talking! The 17 Skills Necessary to Influence Your Boss, Family, Team, or Clients for Improved Results* at https://coachmiguel.leadpages.co/ebook. To schedule a call with me, please visit meetme.so/coachmiguel.

Niki Faldemolaei

Get your complimentary guide *10 Rules to Double Your Business in 90 Days* at http://90days.multicastprofits.com.

Barry Gumaer

For a complimentary Video Messaging Infographic and Video Marketing Systems checklist, go to http://Completeav.net/VideoConnections.html. Barry can also be reached via LinkedIn at https://linkedin.com/in/barrygumaersr and Twitter at https://twitter.com/bgumaer.

Joe Ippolito

Joe can be reached through his websites: http://www.mediamarketingmgmt.com

http://www.jtippolito.com http://www.linkedin.com/in/mediamarketingmanagement

Steve Laurvick

As an executive you cannot underestimate the value of measuring revenue. If correctly implemented, analyzed and deployed, multi-touch attribution models have the potential to ignite sales growth. The impact of integrating your data with a retargeted marketing campaign can have a compounding effect.

To get the *Channel Marketing Agency Multi-Touch Workbook*, text your name and email to: steve@csuite.channelmarketingagency. com. Or go to: http://www.Csuite.ChannelMarketingAgency.com and begin implementing your attribution model right now. Go get the worksheet, give it to your marketing manager, and get them to implement one or more of these models today. Make no mistake – measuring revenue will make for a more successful marketing team.

Melodie Rush

Enjoy a complimentary copy of my international best-selling book *Deliver Webinars Like a Pro* at

http://book.deliverwebinars.com and join my Facebook group https://www.facebook.com/groups/deliverwebinars to learn more about webinars.

Stephen Saber

Check out my free videos, "Marketing Unwrapped," at http://tpniuniversity.tpni.com.

Olivier Taupin and Sharon A.M. MacLean

You're not the type of leader to back down from a challenge. If you need a custom-made plan to transform yourself and your organization into a forward-looking enterprise, we are delighted to help show you the way. Social Media Leadership -The Taupin Model© can be obtained for free at

http://media.instantcustomer.com/22902/0/199_10-steps-social-media-leadership.pdf.

Pat Ziemer

To learn more about Magna Wave for employee health and wellness visit http://www.MagnaWavePEMF.com. For a Free 30-minute Multi-Source strategy call, a $750.00 value, visit http://www.MultiSourceStrategy.com. For web-related services visit http://www.mwmediadesign.com.

Disclaimer

No Warranties

The information in this book is provided "as is" without any representations or warranties, expressed or implied. The Authors and/or Publisher make no representations or warranties in relation to the information and materials provided in this book.

Without prejudice to the generality of the foregoing paragraph, the Authors and/or Publisher do not warrant that:

• the information in this book is complete, true, accurate or non-misleading;

• nothing in this book constitutes, or is meant to constitute, advice of any kind.

Limitations of Liability

The Authors and/or Publisher will not be liable to you (whether under the law of contract, the law of torts or otherwise) in relation to the contents of, or use of, or otherwise in connection with, this book:

• for any direct loss;

• for any indirect, special or consequential loss; or for any business losses, loss of revenue, income, profits or anticipated savings, loss of contracts or business relationships, loss of reputation or goodwill, or loss or corruption of information or data.

Made in the USA
Charleston, SC
18 March 2016